D1500046

Tell Me How I'm Doing

Tell Me How I'm Doing

A Fable About the Importance of
Giving Feedback

Richard L. Williams

AMACOM

American Management Association

New York • Atlanta • Brussels • Chicago • Mexico City • San Francisco
Shanghai • Tokyo • Toronto • Washington, D.C.

Special discounts on bulk quantities of AMACOM books are available to corporations, professional associations, and other organizations. For details, contact Special Sales Department, AMACOM, a division of American Management Association, 1601 Broadway, New York, NY 10019.
Tel.: 212-903-8316. Fax: 212-903-8083.
Web site: www.amacombooks.org

This publication is designed to provide accurate and authoritative information in regard to the subject matter covered. It is sold with the understanding that the publisher is not engaged in rendering legal, accounting, or other professional service. If legal advice or other expert assistance is required, the services of a competent professional person should be sought.

Library of Congress Cataloging-in-Publication Data

Williams, Richard L. (Richard Leonard), 1943–
    Tell me how I'm doing : a fable about the importance of giving feedback / Richard L. Williams.
        p.   cm.
    ISBN 0-8144-0832-X (hardcover)
    1. Communication in management.   2. Feedback (Psychology)
3. Supervision of employees.   4. Employee motivation.   5. Interpersonal communication.   I. Title.

HD30.3.W545   2004
658.3′14—dc22   2004009628

Printing number

10   9   8   7   6   5   4   3   2   1

Dedication

This book is dedicated to my daughter Tracy Morris, who will always be my special Snuggle; to my son Dr. Trevor Williams, who is an inspiration of sacrifice and dedication; to my son Trent Williams, who is always so willing to serve, no matter the cost or inconvenience; to my son Tyler Williams, who motivates me with his hard work in medical school; and to my daughter Tiffany Williams, who is so beautiful and brilliant.

This book is also dedicated to my favorite sons-in-law, Hector and Mike, who are such good friends; and to my three favorite daughters-in-law, Anna, Mendee, and Cherise, who are so much fun to love and tease. And to the growing tribe of grandchildren who make my life so much fun.

Finally, this book is dedicated to my wife, Rhonda, who has taught me so much and remains my best friend and eternal companion.

Contents

Preface

My first introduction to the principles of interpersonal feedback was in graduate school, where I was required to read a classic article by Dr. Hank Karp titled "The Lost Art of Feedback." It's a fairly lengthy discussion on the methods and techniques of delivering supportive and corrective feedback. At first I approached the assignment like most students. I looked for objective material on which I might be tested, along with topics that could show up in classroom discussions. But the deeper I got into the article the more enamored I became with Dr. Karp's insights in effective methods of giving feedback.

After I completed my formal education, I found myself referring back to "The Lost Art of Feedback" every year or so, because it helped me understand the methods of effective interpersonal communication. Then, as a teacher many years later, I resurrected the same article and required my students to read and even be tested on it. One of the teaching methods I used was to administer a ten-item true-or-false pretest to get my students' attention and prepare them for what they were about to experience. Inasmuch as you are about to embark on a similar experience by reading this book, I think it is once again appropriate to administer the same quiz. Let's see how you do.

Feedback Quiz

Circle T or F

T F   1. Supportive feedback reinforces a behavior you like, and corrective feedback is used to indicate that a change is needed.

T F   2. Good performance and appropriate behavior are to be expected, and the only time feedback is really needed is when something goes wrong.

T F   3. If you were forced to give only one kind of feedback, you would be further ahead to use supportive feedback, rather than corrective feedback.

T F   4. If your comments to someone focus on what he or she is doing well, that person becomes more aware of superior performance.

T F   5. When giving corrective feedback to change a behavior, don't let the other person take full responsibility for his or her actions.

T F   6. When giving feedback, you should deal in specifics and focus on specific behaviors, rather than attitudes.

T F   7. Corrective feedback should be used to change a behavior that is ineffective or inappropriate.

T F   8. While not damaging if done properly, corrective feedback is not a particularly pleasant experience. At the least, the person receiving it will probably feel a little defensive or even embarrassed.

T F   9. When giving supportive feedback, specifically describe the behavior and/or results caused by the behavior that you would like the person to repeat.

T F   10. Corrective feedback works best if it's given in specific behavioral terms and as soon as possible after the event.

Scoring the quiz is easy: All of the questions are true, except items two and five, which are false. Having administered this quiz to many classes, I found that most students typically get seven or eight of the ten items correct. The most often missed question is number three. I suppose that is because it's a stretch for most people to believe that giving supportive feedback is actually more important than giving corrective feedback. Too many of us are far too quick to point out someone's mistakes and far too slow to point out what the person has done that is correct. It's been my experience that most managers and parents overwhelm others with a list of perceived mistakes.

Question five asks if people should be required to take "full responsibility" for their behaviors. It's my opinion that far too many parents, and some managers, try to shield people from being responsible for their actions. The long-term consequences of being immune from responsibility can be severe. That's why Dr. Karp feels so strongly about ensuring that people are held accountable for their actions.

As I taught management development and leadership workshops over the years, the concepts presented in this book gradually evolved. At first my teaching began to clarify the basic principles of feedback. And as time went on the metaphor of the feedback bucket was formulated. Technically, every principle taught in this book is a result of either the original article by Dr. Karp or the concepts I learned while teaching workshops. For me, learning feedback has truly been an experience of self-discovery.

One of the most important aspects of *Tell Me How I'm Doing* is that every character in the book is based on a real person. My good friend Marty, who works in Ohio, inspired Scott, the main character. I have been privileged to watch Marty make miraculous life changes like Scott does in this book.

The character of The Abused Woman is based on a true story about another good friend. The remarkable changes to The Abused Woman depicted in this book actually happened.

Still another good friend, Tim, inspired the character Manager in the Hallway. I've known Tim for many years and the challenges described in this book regarding the Manager in the Hallway are very accurate, and unfortunately true.

I believe that the communication skills necessary to be effective at work are almost identical to the communication skills necessary to be effective as a parent or partner at home. For this reason, the techniques described in *Tell Me How I'm Doing* are intended to help in both of those areas. One book editor said to me, "I'm not sure if this is a business book that has application at home, or if it's a book on parenting that has application in business." Whichever it is, the design was deliberate.

Acknowledgments

Whether a book is long or short, there are always many people responsible for its creation, and this book is no exception. *Tell Me How I'm Doing* had its beginnings in the hundreds of workshops that I conducted in many companies and organizations. So the first people to thank are my thousands of students who inspired me to learn more about interpersonal feedback. Without these students and the great organizations they represent, this book would not exist!

There are particular people who played critical roles in this book's development. Some were my teachers, others assisted with the text, others gave me invaluable feedback about the story line, and others offered encouragement to complete the work. These people include Cathy Anderegg, Lyman Baker, Chuck Coonradt, Art Cornwell, Dr. Ian Griggs, John Hanson, Becky Harding, Tim Hartsuck, Rich Jennings, Lorna Johnson, Rick Keeler, Fay Klingler, Craig Mathes, John (Trip) Morris, Clair Naylor, Bob Perschon, John Phillips, Steve Rodgers, Shelley Roth, Dr. Marshall

Sashkin, Marty Schlessel, Ann Whitney, Trent Williams, and Rick Zenobi.

And finally, I would be remiss not to express my appreciation and love to my family for their support during the writing and editing process. My wife, Rhonda, played a particularly critical role of being a sounding board. Without her support and assistance this book would have remained a vague hope in the recesses of my mind.

Tell Me How I'm Doing

The Experiment

"Hey there, you goin'?"

"Yeah, I'd better. I really don't have time, but if I don't go, he'll be on my case."

"Let's get a move on, or we'll be late."

Scott had forgotten about a meeting his boss had scheduled for the managers in his division that morning. He didn't want to go, because he had some things he needed to do. He really didn't have time for the meeting. In fact, he didn't have time for many things lately. The problem was that he had too many problems, both at work and at home.

Moments later his boss said, "Let's get started. We've got a guest coach and I want to give her as much time as I can. We're going to do something that may seem weird to some of you, but if you'll give our coach a chance, I'm sure you'll see how important her message is. I first heard her speak a couple of years ago, but it took a while for her message to sink in. Guess I'm a little slow on this subject."

Scott was thinking, *If it took a while for you to get her message, what are we doing here? I've got a lot of things I could be doing right now.*

Complete This Statement

The coach began. "Thanks for inviting me here today. Let's begin by having you complete this statement: 'The biggest problem with being a manager is to get your people to . . .'"

After a brief pause, a colleague of Scott's replied, "Get them to do what they're supposed to."

Another added, "Without whining or complaining." Several of the managers in the room nodded their agreement to this comment.

Still another colleague said, "I need my people to do it right the first time."

The coach asked, "Let me guess. For the most part your employees know what they're supposed to do?"

"Pretty much," someone responded.

"So I'm curious. If your people know what they know, why do some of them do what they do?"

There was a long silence in the room while everyone pondered the answer. Scott was thinking that the employees who had given him the most trouble that week pretty much knew what they should do, but they fought him at every step. Scott's face must have given his thoughts away because the coach looked at him and asked, "I can see the wheels turning. Tell us what you're thinking."

Caught off guard, Scott said, "I was thinking that no matter how much my people seem to *know*, it's hard to get them to *do* what they need to. I'm not sure if that makes sense."

"Sure it does. It makes so much sense that we're going to spend some time this morning figuring out the answer. I don't like to play games with blame, shame, and guilt, but in a situation where an employee knows *what* to do, *how* to do it, and even *when* to do it—but for some unexplainable reason chooses not to do it—what is the root cause?"

No one answered, so the coach looked at Scott and asked, "What do you think? Who is responsible?"

Scott shook his head and said, "If my employee knows what to do, how to do it, and when to do it, *but then chooses not to do it,* it's the employee's problem."

The coach walked to the center of the room and took a drink of water. She looked in the eyes of the dozen people in the room and said, "What do you think: employee or manager?"

Most of the managers in the room smelled a trap, and those who didn't were unsure of the answer. Scott wasn't sure what she meant, but he was sure that there wasn't any way he was responsible for what his employees refused to do. In fact, Scott was becoming frustrated with this discussion, but he didn't want to be disagreeable with his boss in the room.

Sensing frustration in the room, the coach raised an eyebrow and with a slight smile said, "To answer that question, let me tell you *why* your boss described this presentation as a little 'weird.' But before we do that, let's take a short, five-minute break. There is something I need to do."

The Invisible Man

A few minutes later, as Scott was walking back to the meeting room, his boss stopped him. "Say, Scott, would you do me a favor? The receptionist in the front lobby has an envelope with my name on it. Would you mind getting it for me? It's okay if you're late to the meeting." A bit puzzled, Scott agreed and began walking toward the other end of the building.

Back in the meeting room, the coach quickly closed the door and said, "We're going to conduct an experiment. Scott has been sent on a fictitious errand so that we can set it up. In a minute he'll return with an envelope that your boss asked him to fetch:

That's the fictitious errand. When he returns, I need all of us to completely ignore Scott. We don't look at him. We don't talk to him. If he asks a question, we ignore him. We'll all pretend he isn't here. And we're going to do this for the next hour. We'll have another break in about an hour, so be sure that you don't engage or communicate with him in any way during that break. Remember, for an hour he doesn't exist. After the next break we'll debrief Scott to see what he noticed and how he felt about being ignored. Any questions? Good. Now let's begin so he won't suspect anything when he returns."

A minute later Scott walked into the room and tried to hand the envelope to his boss, but the boss didn't reach out to take it; he just looked straight ahead at the coach. Confused, Scott placed it on the table near his boss and returned to his seat.

The coach was telling a story about a man who, after he was promoted to a supervisory position, became so ineffective in dealing with his employees that he later lost his job. His employees complained that the new supervisor overly criticized and complained to the point that they lost their motivation to perform. The coach looked up from her notes and asked, "What do you think? Can criticism, complaining, or even sarcasm motivate employees to work harder?"

No one said a word. There was total silence. Finally, Scott raised his hand; he wanted to clarify something. But the coach ignored his upraised hand and no one looked his way. After a few seconds of silence, the coach continued, "It looks as though we're not sure of the answer."

She walked to a position directly in front of Scott. Without looking at him, she continued, "When someone is critical or sarcastic to you, how motivated does that make you? When someone ignores you, how much harder do you work? Think about it."

Again Scott raised his hand—a little higher this time. In fact, his hand was now right in front of the coach's face. But still she ignored him. Scott looked around the room at a dozen of his friends and colleagues, but no one looked at him. It was as if he had disappeared. *What is going on?* he thought.

An hour later the coach gave another break. Scott walked up to his close friend, the person he usually ate lunch with and someone he had known and worked with for the past five years. Scott was upset—something was going on, and he didn't like it! "What's going on?" he asked. But his friend looked right through him and walked out of the room; he didn't seem to see Scott. *If this is a joke, it's not funny!*

The meeting resumed with Scott's arms folded tightly across his chest and his face set like concrete. He was thinking that there were only two possibilities: either a space alien had made him invisible, or a dozen people, some close friends, had made him the victim of a sadistic game. Either way, he didn't like it and was feeling frustrated and felt like going back to his office to do something productive.

"Something the matter, Scott?" the coach finally asked.

"Something is going on, but I don't know what!" replied Scott.

"So what do you think is going on?" she continued.

"You're all playing some kind of a game."

Sensing his frustration, she smiled and said, "Scott, we were indeed playing a game. Your boss volunteered you for an important demonstration, because you know these people well and he thought you could take a little ribbing. I hope he was correct."

"So what's this all about?" he asked.

"Scott, for the past hour everyone in this room has denied you any type of feedback whatsoever. I instructed your colleagues to totally ignore you. None of us, myself included, could look at or speak to you. I realize it's an unusual demonstration, but I needed someone to experience firsthand what happens in the heart of a person who is denied feedback. So now I need you to tell us what you felt and how long it took you to notice that something was different."

Scott paused and said, "Well, I could tell as soon as I walked in the room. Nobody looked at me. Nobody responded in any way."

"And you felt . . ." the coach prompted.

"I felt awful, especially on the break when people looked straight through me. I knew something was wrong, but I couldn't figure out what it was."

"So, Scott, how important is feedback in your life?"

"If it was feedback that was missing, it's really important."

The coach took a couple of steps toward Scott and said, "And if you as an employee were denied feedback, totally or even partially, in this organization, for an hour, a week, or even longer, how productive would you be at performing your job responsibilities?"

The managers in the room noticed a pained look on Scott's face. It was apparent that something had just struck him. He paused a few seconds and replied, "Not very."

Also having noticed Scott's reaction, the coach pursued her thought and asked, "If you were denied feedback, much like you were for the past hour in this room, how responsible, loyal, or trustworthy would you be to this organization? Would your productivity be high, or low? How much initiative would you demonstrate in your job? How much morale would you have? And how likely would you be to turn down a job offer to go someplace else?"

The coach had hit too close to home for Scott. He felt almost paralyzed as he sat trying to find the right words to answer her questions. Finally, he conceded her questions and merely said, "Feedback is really important, isn't it?"

"That's right, Scott, feedback is important to all of us. It's the foundation of all interpersonal relationships. It determines how people think, how they feel, how they react to others, and to a large extent, it determines how people act in their daily responsibilities."

The coach paused while she looked over the group of managers to ensure that her message was having the impact she intended. Then she looked back toward Scott and continued, "Organizations like this one spend a great deal of time, effort, and money instituting programs to increase and maintain employee productivity. All you have to do is scan the business section of any bookstore and you'll find dozens of books intended to get employees to work more efficiently and effectively. Now I'm not putting those books down by any means, but what I want you to understand is that at the foundation of all worker productivity is a basic need for interpersonal feedback. Without it people tend to demonstrate problems in the workplace: the types of problems that we spend far too much money and resources on trying to solve. And with appropriate feedback people tend to do the things that those books on the shelves attempt to describe."

The coach nodded at her own comment and added, "So, how important is feedback to each of us? Well, let's just say that it's the lifeblood for every person in this room and every mentally healthy person in this organization."

There was an eerie silence in the room as the significance of what the coach had said began to sink in. It was obvious that the managers were taking personal inventory of their own feedback style. A couple of managers looked down at their notes to avoid the coach's eyes. One manager nervously glanced at her watch. Scott stared blankly at a wall and then at the coach.

With her message made, the coach made a concluding comment. "Thanks for your attendance this morning. I appreciate your participation. I especially appreciate Scott being our test subject. I hope you'll all give him an extra dose of feedback to hopefully compensate for what we did to him. Is that okay Scott?"

"I'll be okay," Scott replied.

"In our next class we'll continue our discussion on feedback and find out exactly how important it is to everyone, including our employees and family members."

As people were leaving, the coach walked over to Scott and said, "I really hope you are okay. The envelope exercise can be a pretty unnerving demonstration."

Scott nodded that he was okay.

"Now that you've experienced the power of feedback first-hand, how many of the problems you experience with employees and perhaps your family members are related to your style of giving feedback?"

Stunned, Scott replied, "I've never thought about it."

To which the coach merely said, "Perhaps before our next class you'll have an opportunity to give it some thought. The answer may surprise you."

Throughout that day, and for several days that followed, Scott found himself reflecting upon the coach's questions. At first he conceded that perhaps a few of the problems with his employees could be related to his failure to "give good feedback," as she called it. But there wasn't any way that most of his problems were caused by it. As the days rolled on, he began to question that belief.

The Wake-Up Call

From: Scott
Reply-To: Scott@acompany.com
To: <Coach@consultingcompany.com
Subject: Your Question at Our First Session

I realize that our next training session isn't until next week, but I can't get your last question out of my mind. You asked if there was any connection between the problems I've been having with my employees and the way I give them feedback. And you hinted that the same thing might be true with my family as well. My first reaction was there was no connection, and that I give feedback just fine. But I've been thinking about how I felt during that hour when nobody was talking to me and how I reacted to being denied feedback. Now I'm not so sure. What's the answer? Is there a relationship?

From: Coach
Reply-To: Coach@consultingcompany.com
To: <Scott@acompany.com
Subject: Your Message This Morning

I'm pleased you've been thinking about our discussion. Before we get to your question, you need to understand the importance of feedback—to both employees and family members.

Actually, interpersonal feedback is a critical nutrient of life. Let me explain. We can only go a few minutes without air, a few days without water, and a few weeks without food. Those are the three most important physiological nutrients of life for humans. But most people don't realize that for a mentally healthy person the fourth most important nutrient of life is interpersonal feedback. That's right, feedback is in a similar category as the three physiological nutrients.

As you learned in our first class, when a person is denied feedback for even an hour, that person can not only *feel* the results of the denial, but that person is likely to *respond* with unproductive and/or inappropriate behaviors. So if your employees aren't producing like they should, or if you see inappropriate behaviors from them, it's possible that the underlying cause is the quality and/or quantity of feedback they are receiving, possibly from you. The same thing is most likely true at home as well. Does that help?

From: Scott
Reply-To: Scott@acompany.com
To: <Coach@consultingcompany.com
Subject: Feedback

I've never considered that my feedback could have that much impact on other people. It's a lot to take in all at once.

I have an employee whose name is Jerry. He used to be my best producer, so I basically left him alone to do his own thing. I thought if I got out of his way he would continue producing for me. But over the last several months Jerry's production has dropped by almost 35 percent and his follow-through has gone down the drain. I jumped all over him and he immediately got better, but only for about a week or so. Then he was back to the same problems. So I jumped on him again, and he got better; but again, it was only for a day or so. It seems that if I get on his case he gets better. But for some reason he can't do it by himself like he used to. And I don't have enough time to ride his case every day. So is this problem related to feedback? What should I do?

From: Coach
Reply-To: Coach@consultingcompany.com
To: <Scott@acompany.com
Subject: Jerry

Let me see if I understand. Jerry was a "great producer," which probably made him one of your best employees. For that distinction you reduced the amount of feedback you gave him by leaving him alone under the pretense of "not getting in his way." Then the quantity and quality of his performance dramatically eroded, so you increased the amount of critical feedback, which only temporarily solved the problem. And you want to know how to get him back to the level of performance he was at a year ago. You tell me, what's wrong with this picture?

From: Scott
Reply-To: Scott@acompany.com
To: <Coach@consultingcompany.com
Subject: Jerry's Feedback

It sounds like you are saying it was a mistake to leave him alone when he was doing well. I think I see the problem with that, but are you also saying that I shouldn't reprimand an employee whose performance falls off by 35 percent? If you don't chew out bad employees, what are you supposed to do, pat them on the back?

From: Coach
Reply-To: Coach@consultingcompany.com
To: <Scott@acompany.com
Subject: Feedback

A very wise person once said that it's insane to continue doing something that doesn't work, expecting the results to get better. If what you are doing isn't working and it would be insane to expect improvement while continuing with the same strategy, what can you do to make the situation better?

Are you ready to understand the power of feedback and how it can make you more effective and your life a lot more enjoyable? By the way, are you ready to make things better at home, too?

From: Scott
Reply-To: Scott@acompany.com
To: <Coach@consultingcompany.com
Subject: My Insanity!

I hope I'm not insane! Okay, I give up. I'm ready. How can I improve my feedback?

Next Class with the Coach

The same group of managers assembled in the meeting room, but before the class began there were a few friendly jabs and even apologies directed at Scott. Scott's boss teased him, saying, "Hey, Scott, you wanna get an envelope for me?" Everyone laughed, including Scott, for he felt more at ease with the group than he had in the previous meeting.

Scott's boss asked everyone to be seated and then said, "Thanks for coming back to this next class. I appreciate your attendance and I'm sure we'll all learn more about this important topic. So let me turn the time over to our coach."

The coach had arranged the chairs around tables in a U formation so that the managers could see each other. She had a small table at the head of the U, where she placed her notes. After again thanking the boss for his invitation to the company, the coach picked up a small stack of light gray papers from the front table and held them for the managers to see. "I'd like to begin with this exercise. You might think of it as a questionnaire, but technically it's an instrument that quantifies your current manner and techniques of giving feedback to others. Now, this instrument focuses primarily on how you give feedback at work, but in future classes we'll spend some time on how to give feedback at home. That's because the ability to give feedback at work and at home are connected and equally important."

The Feedback Instrument

The coach began passing an instrument to each manager and continued, "Please don't consider this a test, because it's not. All of us have strengths and weaknesses. But before we can lessen the impact of our weaknesses, we must first know what they are. That's where this instrument comes in. After you take it and we score the results, you'll be aware of areas where improvement is needed. Equally important, you'll also know your personal strengths in giving feedback."

Twenty minutes later each manager held a graph that illustrated his or her strengths and weaknesses in giving feedback in ten areas, or "dimensions," as they are called in the instrument.

1. Have a plan.

2. Be specific.

3. Focus on behaviors.

4. Time and place.

5. Balanced feedback.

6. Relevant feedback.

7. Effective techniques.

8. Effective style.

9. Describe feelings.

10. Listening skills.

A few of the managers who finished scoring their instrument early began comparing their results. As the remaining managers completed the scoring process, the coach said, "Now that you have an idea of your current feedback skills, let's take a look at the ten dimensions."

The Ten Dimensions

The coach picked up an instrument and after pausing to look at it for a few seconds said, "The ten dimensions are constructed to give an overview or comprehensive perspective of feedback. In future training sessions we'll discuss each of these topics in more detail. For now, as I briefly define each dimension, why don't you follow along on your instrument? In fact, if you want to make a note or two, that will be fine. So turn to the page in your instrument that lists the ten dimensions."

The coach paused for a few seconds while the managers opened their questionnaires. When they were ready, she continued. "The first dimension is 'Have a plan.' It means to give your feedback some preparatory thought and then deliver it with clear examples and have a solution in mind. It also means to be flexible to the needs and wants of the recipient. The second dimension is 'Be specific,' which means to know what actually happened and then to use clear, understandable examples without having to guess. The third dimension is 'Focus on behaviors.' Effective feedback doesn't deal with personalities, attitudes, or labels. It focuses on specific behaviors that can be seen or measured. The fourth dimension is 'Time and place,' which deals with how soon the feedback is given and where. Feedback should be given as soon after the event as possible, hopefully in a low-stress situation, and corrective feedback should never be given in public. 'Balanced feedback,' is the next dimension, and it refers to the balance between giving supportive versus corrective feedback. As you'll see in future training sessions, too many managers are out of balance in favor of giving corrective feedback. So this dimension is a key indicator in how you are currently doing in your feedback."

The coach looked up from her instrument and glanced around the room. She asked, "Are there any questions so far?"

"Should I be concerned if I didn't score very well on that last dimension?" a manager asked.

"I wouldn't be overly concerned," the coach cautioned, "It's common. And that's why we are here. These classes are designed to help us learn how to better deliver feedback so that we can become more effective."

After a short pause she continued. "The sixth dimension is 'Relevant feedback.' It means when giving feedback we shouldn't lose our cool or overreact. It's important to be objective and stay calm. Events from the here and now are far more relevant than events long ago. The seventh dimension of the instrument has to do with using 'Effective techniques.' These include such things as getting to the point, using eye contact, and focusing on one major issue. 'Effective style,' is the eighth dimension, which refers to creating a personal approach of delivering feedback. An effective style takes time to develop and includes not giving advice unless the person asks for it. The next dimension is 'Describe feelings,' which can be difficult for some people who are uncomfortable in expressing their own feelings. As we'll see in a later training session, our feelings are important and they can be powerful and have impact when coupled with a feedback message. The final dimension is 'Listening skills.' This consists of encouraging the other person to express his or her opinions and then really hearing what is said. Another part of effective listening is the ability to ask open-ended questions that cause the other person to express important opinions."

The coach placed the instrument on the table in front of her and looked at the group. Teasingly she asked, "That was quite a mouthful of psychobabble, wasn't it? But you needed those ten definitions before we look at your scores, or they wouldn't make much sense. So, shall we look at your scores?"

Each manager could compare his or her individual results on the ten dimensions against a shaded area, or what the instrument indicated as an "ideal score." So, in the first dimension of "Have a plan," a manager could see his or her own score and then compare that score against an average. As the coach explained how to interpret the scores, there were a few raised eyebrows and comments from the managers.

"Now that you understand how this works," the coach explained, "let's see if we can apply the instrument to how we actually give feedback."

Opportunity for Improvement (OFI)

The coach took a few steps toward a manager with blonde, curly hair who was sitting to the coach's left. She stopped in front of the manager and asked, "So in which of the ten dimensions did you score best?"

The manager looked down at the graph he had drawn to score the instrument and said, "I did about the same in number two, 'Be specific,' and number four, 'Time and place.'"

The coach nodded and then asked, "Let me make sure I phrase this in a politically correct manner. In which dimension do your scores indicate that you could use the most improvement?"

With a smile on his face, the manager looked around the room at his colleagues and replied, "That's a nice way of asking where I screw up the most, isn't it?"

There were several chuckles from the managers, but they all were well aware that each of them had several low scores as well. The coach smiled and responded, "Let's just say that on instruments like this one, each of us will usually have what I call an OFI, or opportunity for improvement. An OFI is merely an area where, if we were to gain some improvement, we would make ourselves more effective in accomplishing our objectives. So tell us one of your opportunities for improvement."

The manager looked down again at his graph and said, "I scored lowest in number five, 'Balanced feedback.'"

"And why do you think that balancing supportive and corrective feedback is your greatest OFI?"

The manager looked up from his graph and turned his head

slightly from side to side as he considered the question. After a brief pause, he responded, "I'm a do-it-now type of guy. I expect things to get done when they are supposed to get done. And when someone comes through and things get done, I often forget to express my appreciation. I guess that's because I don't think about it."

The coach looked directly at him and asked, "And what do you do if things don't happen exactly as you expect?"

"I think that's probably the problem and why I was invited to this class. I'm quick to point out what's wrong, but not so quick to point out what's right. I suspect that's the reason I didn't score very well in the balanced feedback category."

"That's a very good observation. And I suspect that your self-analysis is probably right on target."

The coach walked back to the front of the room and continued her explanation of the feedback instrument. "I'd like each of you to look at the scoring graph that you made. Then, circle the dots on the two dimensions in which you scored the highest, and put a box or square around the two dots on the dimensions that are your OFIs, or opportunities for improvement. As we go through the process of learning effective techniques of giving feedback, I would like you to refer back to this exercise as a reminder of your strengths and OFIs."[1]

The coach paused a few seconds to ensure that there were no

1. Note to the reader: Two copies of the instrument used by the coach, Feedback Assessment Inventory, are contained in the appendix. You may want to complete the instrument at this point to assess your own feedback skills. As the coach asked the managers to do, circle your two highest strengths and place a box or square around your two OFIs. Then you can occasionally refer back to the instrument as you continue improving your feedback.

You may wish to retake the instrument three to six months after reading this book and practicing the principles of feedback. By comparing your score from the first instrument to the second one, you could observe your improvement and identify areas for future development.

questions and then added, "Let's take a short break and then we'll begin the process of learning how to give feedback that really works."

Five Things to Know About Feedback

After the managers returned from the break, the coach said, "Before we get to what you can do to improve your feedback to others, there are five things you first need to understand about feedback."

The coach walked to the left side of the U formation of tables where a manager dressed in a dark suit was seated. She looked at him and said, "Number one: The quality of any relationship, business or personal, is dependent on the quality and quantity of feedback each person receives from the other. If the feedback is poor, so is the relationship. If the feedback is critical or abusive, so is the relationship. But, if the feedback is positive, the relationship can be, too."

Then she walked a few feet down the U and stopped in front of a woman who was wearing a beige coat and matching skirt. She smiled at the manager and began, "Number two: Executives, managers, and even line supervisors can become blinded to the fact that social pleasantries are an important type of feedback. Scott can testify what happens in the heart of a person who is denied feedback, even for only an hour. So saying to an employee, 'Good morning, Ann, how was your weekend?' is important feedback. What could be viewed by some people as irrelevant or unnecessary chitchat is actually very important feedback to most people. This is true for your employees, colleagues, and your family members at home, too."

The coach then walked to the back side of the U formation and stopped in front of the boss. She looked him directly in the eye and smiled. "Number three: Eye contact with an employee, boss, colleague, or family member is a type of feedback to that person. When we fail to make eye contact with someone, we are in essence denying that person a form of feedback. We are saying to that person, 'You aren't important enough for me to bother giving you brief eye contact.' In our Western culture, effective feedback must include at least brief eye contact."

Breaking off her eye contact with the boss, the coach walked a few steps up the right side of the tables and stopped in front of a tall, heavyset manager. Looking at him she said, "The fourth thing we need to know about feedback is that some people require more feedback than others. We call these people high maintenance because they demand so much of our time. Far too often, we shy away from giving these people any feedback at all, because we are afraid the more we give the more they will want. But in reality, by denying a high-maintenance person feedback, we actually make the situation worse, not better."

The coach then continued up the right side of the tables toward the front of the room. She stopped in front of Scott and poured a little more soda from a can into his glass and said, "Now we'll test the strength of our relationship. Number five: Withholding feedback from someone is a type of psychological punishment. Scott is a witness to this fact! He experienced, firsthand, the emotional pain that can be inflicted when feedback is withheld. Because it can be so painful when denied, it can also be so powerful when properly applied. I think Scott got that message in our last class. I hope the rest of you will pay close attention to the lesson he learned in that experience. That's what this is all about!"

The coach broke her concentration and asked Scott, "Are we teasing you too much, or are you getting used to the attention?"

Scott smiled and said, "I can't say that I'm not getting enough attention in these classes. But let me ask you a question. I've never thought that social pleasantries such as saying 'good morning,' or giving eye contact were important. Quite frankly, I do them if I think about it, or if it's convenient. I think I can speak for all of us here, but in this company we tend to be so busy that those things often get ignored. How come they are so important?"

She poured some water into a glass and, after taking a sip, said, "Perhaps this story will answer your question. A few years ago I met with the CEO of a manufacturing company to discuss the problems he was experiencing in his company. He told me he had three concerns. The first was that overall productivity in the plant had gone down by 14 percent in the past two years, which coincided with his appointment as CEO. The second concern was that he sensed his employees didn't trust him. He said people didn't volunteer information and even looked at him suspiciously. And the third concern was that he felt his employees responded to him more out of fear than respect or teamwork.

"A little while later, as we toured the plant, I saw firsthand the cause of at least part of the problem. We frequently encountered his employees in the hallways and production areas. But as we did, the CEO was so focused on me and explaining the plant that he ignored almost everyone who greeted him or looked at him for feedback. I'll never forget the look on a worker's face after she said, 'Good morning,' and was summarily ignored. Her face said, 'What do I have to do to get a response in this place?'"

The coach leaned against her table and continued the story. "I didn't count how many employees he ignored that morning, but it was at least a dozen. He had a dozen opportunities to relate to his employees and give them feedback, but instead, he came across as uncaring, unconcerned, aloof, and possibly even arrogant.

"Later that day when we were back in his office, he told me, 'I just don't know what my people expect. I'm baffled.' So I asked him about our tour earlier that morning; I particularly mentioned the employee we had passed in the breezeway between two buildings. And with a puzzled look on his face, he asked, 'What employee?' His powers of concentration were so strong that he hadn't even seen her, even though she had passed within a few feet of us."

The coach took another sip of water and shook her head slightly from side to side. With a touch of emotion in her voice she said, "So I described the look on that employee's face and what I felt her look said and then asked, 'If you were an employee working for someone who wouldn't even look at you or respond to a hello, how much would you trust that person? How much extra effort would you give to increase or sustain your productivity? And would you mostly fear or respect that person?'"

Pausing a few seconds for her story to have its impact, the coach concluded, "He got the point, but it took several coaching sessions over several months before he was able to relate more effectively with his employees."

The coach turned to Scott and asked, "Now do you see the importance of what we call social pleasantries?"

Without saying anything, Scott merely nodded. He got the message, and so did the other managers.

Trouble Concentrating

The class continued for a while longer, but Scott had difficulty focusing on the subject. Too many of the things the coach had said that morning had hit too close to home. He was glad now that his boss had selected him to be the victim of the experiment in the last class. If he hadn't experienced the pain firsthand, perhaps he wouldn't have gained the insight he had received this morning. It was that insight that was giving him trouble concentrating.

The class ended a while later and Scott found himself being drawn toward the coach. He knew he needed to tell her something. She was gathering her materials and placing them in a briefcase when Scott said, "That's some story about the CEO. I'm afraid I've been guilty of the same thing around here. I'm going to have to pay more attention to how I treat my employees. Especially the social pleasantries, as you call them."

The coach stopped what she was doing and looked directly at Scott. She nodded slightly and asked, "You say you could do better at work. How much better could you do at home, too?"

Scott had to catch himself from falling down! He found it difficult to say anything, but when he had sufficiently recovered, he asked, "How did you know I've been having problems at home, too?"

The coach resumed packing her teaching materials and replied, "Let's just say that I had a strong suspicion. We'll find some time later, because I can probably help you there, too."

Scott's head was spinning as he walked back to his office.

CHAPTER 3

The Feedback Bucket

"It's good to see you again. I've been looking forward to this meeting; it's one of my favorite parts of the process," began the coach. The managers had once again assembled in the meeting room for their next session with the coach. She had obviously arrived early to set up the room with several props.

"This morning we're going to learn one of the most important lessons I know. It's so important that many of you will pick up on an unusual metaphor that we will discuss and use it for many years to come."

The Metaphor

There were two plastic buckets on the table at the front of the room. The coach picked up the smaller of the two buckets, which was about 10 inches in diameter and had a handle on top. She held the bucket up for everyone to see. "This is my feedback bucket," she began. "It's in my heart and each time someone gives me any type of feedback, positive or negative, it goes into my bucket. Each of you has a feedback bucket in your heart as well. And feedback directed to you goes in your bucket."

The coach walked a few steps closer to the first row of chairs, paused for a few seconds, and then continued. "The problem is that our buckets have holes in the bottom." She tilted her bucket so everyone could see that it had several holes in the bottom. Some holes were quite small, but a few were fairly large.

Then she walked back to the table and dipped a measuring cup into the larger bucket, which was filled with water. Holding the measuring cup in one hand for everyone to see, and her feedback bucket in her other hand, she slowly poured the water into her feedback bucket. The water began leaking through the holes in the bottom. "When someone gives me feedback, it goes into my bucket and I respond in particular ways," she explained. "The problem is that the feedback leaks out, because of the holes in the bottom. So if I don't receive additional feedback, my bucket will drain dry over time." She paused while the last of the water she had poured into her bucket leaked into the larger bucket on the table. With the water gone from her feedback bucket, she tilted it once again to show that it was empty. "And that," she said, "is the metaphor of the feedback bucket."

Holes in the Bucket

After placing the buckets back on the table and wiping up a little water that had spilled, the coach looked at Scott and asked, "Scott, how many holes do you have in your bucket?"

Scott smiled and responded, "Quite a few, I guess."

"Perhaps," she said. "Where did they come from?"

He thought for a few seconds and said, "I probably drilled a few myself, and maybe some were put there by other people."

The coach nodded. "Very good insight."

Then Scott continued, "I think I took a shotgun to the bucket of one of my employees a few months ago."

"Tell us about that."

Scott shrugged his shoulders, took a quick glance at his boss, and began. "There's this guy who a year ago was one of my best employees. Instead of filling his bucket with positive feedback, I ignored him, thinking he knew how good he was and how much I appreciated him. Then I guess his bucket ran dry and his production declined. I reacted by being critical. I suppose that's called critical feedback, but it only caused a temporary improvement. Then his production declined again. In these last few weeks since these classes started I've just begun to understand that I may be responsible for what happened."

The coach nodded her agreement. "I hope you all heard what Scott said. Perhaps he is responsible, but I believe that positive deposits into that employee's feedback bucket could once again make him a productive employee. Scott, we'll make that an assignment for you. Okay?"

Agreeing, Scott said, "I've already started."

Team Meetings

After the class returned from a break, the coach said that she had been doing most of the talking and it was now their turn to earn the donuts they had eaten during the break. "Here's what I would like you to do," she explained. "I'm going to divide the class into three teams and you'll have twenty minutes to answer the question that appears on a card that I'll give you. Appoint a spokesperson and that person will have up to five minutes to teach the other two teams what you learned during your team meeting. Here are your team assignments."

The members of each team gathered together in different corners of the room to study and discuss their assignment. Twenty minutes later the first spokesperson stood to give her report. "Our team was asked the question, 'How do holes get in our buckets in the first place?' We agreed that all of us have holes—some are little pinpricks and some can be quite huge. We also agreed that some of the holes can be in a state of flux, meaning that to a certain extent they can vary in size as we progress through life. But now to the question of how they get there in the first place."

The spokesperson went to a whiteboard at the front of the room and wrote the words *INTERNAL* and *EXTERNAL* in large block letters. She turned back to the class. "Our first point is that holes come from internal and external sources. Obviously, internal means that some of the holes are caused by our own actions, or our failure to act. This means that we can drill a hole in our own bucket. One of our team members said that self-destructive people spend too much time blasting holes in their own bucket."

She put a check mark by *INTERNAL* on the board and then pointed at *EXTERNAL*. "We had a lively discussion, to say the least, about who, besides ourselves, shoots holes in our buckets. We didn't have enough time to decide if we can actually stop someone from shooting a hole, but I personally think we can, at least to some extent."

She wrote the numbers 1, 2, 3, 4, and 5 below *EXTERNAL* and continued. "We made a list of the five most common people who put holes in our buckets."

She wrote *Parents* next to number 1. "The first is parents

Figure 3-1. Sources of holes in a feedback bucket.

INTERNAL:
    1. Ourselves

EXTERNAL:
    1. Parents
    2. Friends
    3. Family
    4. Supervisors
    5. Work associates

because we think the way a person is parented has a lot to do with how many holes get drilled as children grow up."

Next she wrote *Friends*. "The second source is friends because the people we associate with as we grow up, and also as adults, have a big impact on the holes, too."

Then she wrote the word *Family* next to number 3. "The third is family because even the best families seem to have such things as sibling rivalry, competition, disagreements, arguments, and even all-out wars on occasion. And don't forget what a spouse can do to fill or empty a bucket.

"The fourth source is *Supervisors*. A few minutes ago Scott said—how did you put it? You said you blasted an employee's bucket with a shotgun? Well, whether it is intentional or not, as managers we can add holes by how we act and what we say— maybe by what we don't say, too.

"We called our fifth source *Work associates,* the people we work with. How we communicate with each other in our daily conversations includes various forms of feedback. The quality of those conversations can either drill new holes or plug up a few old ones. So that's our report."

Next, the second spokesperson announced, "We were given two questions: 'How do people behave when their buckets are empty?' and 'What clues tell us a person's bucket is empty?' The first thing our team agreed on is that most people don't consciously know when their bucket is empty. It's something we can't recognize because most of us don't understand it. And it's a feeling or an emotion; being able to pinpoint emotions is difficult for most people."

The second spokesperson glanced at a couple of his team members and continued. "Something else we talked about is that even if a person knew that his or her 'bucket gauge' was on empty, it would be highly unlikely that the person would ask for feedback—men especially wouldn't ask, because it wouldn't be macho. It would show weakness. If women are the better communicators, like some people say, and if they are more intuitive, again like some people say, then maybe women would be better suited to know when their bucket was empty, and maybe they might be more able to ask for help. But we weren't really sure about that."

Referring to his notes, he added, "We came up with a few ways that might indicate that a person's bucket was low, or even empty. Maybe I'd better list them on the board so you don't think the first team got the best of us."

He walked to the whiteboard and printed *EMPTY BUCKET* near the top. Then he listed the numbers 1, 2, 3, and 4 below it and printed *Low production/performance* next to number 1. "We felt that a person's work performance is tied directly to the amount of feedback in his or her bucket. It doesn't mean that people stop working when their buckets are empty, but we believe that sustained performance requires at least a minimal amount of feedback in the bucket."

He printed *Can't get along with others* next to number 2. "This one was an eye-opener for me. I've never considered that the ability to get along peaceably with coworkers might be related to how much feedback people are receiving. I've got two people in my department right now who just can't get along with each other. But, you know, I haven't done much bucket filling with either of these people. So maybe it's time I stop ignoring them and see if more feedback from me will help them get along better with each other.

"The third thing we came up with is *Demonstrates low initia-*

Figure 3-2. Clues to empty-bucket behaviors.

EMPTY BUCKET:
1. Low production/performance
2. Can't get along with others
3. Demonstrates low initiative
4. Body language signals

tive. For example, people with empty buckets are more prone to be followers at best, rather than take the initiative and be leaders. Another example of initiative is making decisions. In this company we've had many discussions about getting our employees to step up to the plate and make decisions. It's a big deal around here. Fuller buckets could help our people do that."

After printing *Body language signals* next to number 4 on the board, the spokesperson said, "The final thing we came up with is body language. Nobody on our team is an expert on body language, but we all agreed that body language must be one of the most obvious signals of an empty bucket. I watched Scott in our first class when we all ignored him. It was obvious by his body language that he didn't like what was going on."

The spokesperson glanced at Scott and then continued, "In this company we tend to be so busy driving profit to the bottom line that we don't pay much attention to what our people are trying to tell us by how they act. It doesn't sound difficult, so I guess we need to just pay more attention to what people are saying to us through their body language."

After a short break, the third spokesperson began her team's presentation by reading their assignment to the class. "Our card asked, 'What can be done to plug up holes in a person's bucket?'" She walked to the whiteboard and said, "It looks like the precedent has been set and it includes me writing on this board. We can't have the best team looking inferior to the other teams, can we?"

She held up the dry-erase marker and asked, "Does this magic marker have spell check?"

"We identified five things that can plug up holes. The first is *Develop emotional maturity.* There's only so much a manager can do to improve an employee's emotional maturity, but we felt that it needed to be included in our list anyway. I don't know if anyone here has read Daniel Goleman's book *Emotional Intelligence*, but I highly recommend it. I think it should be a prerequisite to being

Figure 3-3. Methods to plug holes in a bucket.

HOW TO PLUG HOLES:
1. Develop emotional maturity.
2. Give quality feedback.
3. Offer praise/recognition.
4. Celebrate achievements.
5. Delegate decision making.

a boss or a parent. The second thing on our list is *Give quality feedback*. We believe that high-quality feedback can plug up a few holes. Our third one is *Offer praise and recognition*. It seems to us that employees who receive appropriate and timely praise and recognition for their contributions to the company would feel better about themselves. And that could plug up a hole or two. A lot of books have been written about how to recognize employees, but I'm not sure that we do enough recognition around here. The fourth thing we came up with is to help our employees *Celebrate achievements*. As managers we get stuck thinking that results are expected, so we don't need to celebrate individual successes. But we really need to. The last thing we came up with is *Delegate decision making*. We thought that when decision making is delegated to hourly employees they feel more involved with what's going on and that has to influence a hole or two in their buckets. So that's what we came up with."

The third spokesperson walked back to her chair, but as she was about to sit down, she paused and turned toward the coach and said, "There was one more thing. Something came up in our discussion that we didn't know. We weren't sure if once a hole was drilled in a person's bucket it could ever be permanently repaired. Does that make sense? I guess I'm asking if a hole is always going to leak. We weren't sure."

The coach pulled a chair to the front of the room and sat down. Looking first at the spokesperson and then glancing at several other class members she asked, "So once you've done what you can to repair a hole with the best feedback possible, you want to know how long the patch will last? Is that your question?"

"Yes." The spokesperson replied. "We're not really sure."

"It's a common question. And there frankly isn't any clear-cut answer, because every person, and every hole, and every situation is a little different. But I can give you a few basic guidelines. The technical answer is that once a hole has been drilled in a person's feedback bucket it can only be patched in a way that it is likely to leak again over time. Now, that leak may only be a small drip, or the entire patch could possibly fall apart. The value of the patch depends on the quality of the feedback given and how well the feedback is received by the person. And as you can perhaps imagine, it's much easier to patch small holes and very difficult to patch large ones. Does that help?"

Nodding, the third spokesperson replied, "It does. It's kind of what I was thinking. A small pinprick could be patched and might stay patched indefinitely, but a huge hole might spring a leak after a while. That does make sense to me."

"I wish I could offer a guarantee that carefully worded supportive feedback would permanently patch a hole, but I can't. There are just too many variables. But I can tell you from many years of experience that if you practice the principles of feedback you'll learn in these classes, you'll be able to provide patches to holes that will minimize potential leaks. I am convinced of that."

An Unexpected Question

The coach thanked the teams for their reports and suggestions. She challenged everyone to consider what the teams had said. The meeting was adjourned after a few additional comments. As people were leaving the room, Scott stopped to say, "Thanks for the class—I'm learning a lot. I think it's helping."

With a smile the coach replied, "Well, thank you for the supportive feedback. My bucket gets empty sometimes, too. By the way, how full is your wife's bucket these days?"

Puzzled, Scott asked, "How did you know I'm married?"

"The ring on your finger," replied the coach.

Scott absently looked at his ring finger and began turning the ring with the fingers on his right hand. "You don't miss much, do you?"

Sensing a hurt in his voice, the coach explained, "A wise person once said that leaders who are effective at work usually were first effective at home. You are having problems at work, so it was a safe bet that you are also having problems at home, too. Another safe bet would be that the causes are similar."

In a fraction of a second, several painful images of his wife and children flashed through Scott's mind. The look on his face said, "I'm not ready for this discussion yet."

Realizing that this conversation would have to take place another day, the coach added, "Before we have that talk, why don't you go fill your wife's bucket. It'll make our discussion considerably shorter and it will most likely have a positive impact on Jerry, too."

"How could filling my wife's bucket have an impact on Jerry?" asked Scott.

"Give it a try. I think you'll be surprised what can happen when you improve the feedback in one aspect of your life," replied the coach.

"I've got to think about that," replied Scott.

Types of Feedback

From: Scott
Reply-To: Scott@acompany.com
To: <Coach@consultingcompany.com
Subject: Good News & Bad News

I'm sure I haven't mentioned this before, but my wife and I have two children: a ten-year-old girl and a six-year-old boy. You were right the other day. Things haven't been going very well at home. So I've been working on my son's bucket, because it was obviously empty. The first night we sat down after dinner and I told him what I like about him. I told him that I like the way he catches a baseball, that I like the way he helps me mow the lawn, that I like his sense of humor, and that I like his smile. They were just simple comments, but his reaction was incredible! It took me a couple of minutes to put something in his bucket, but he was my shadow for the rest of the night. Then at bedtime he wanted me to read him a story. That's been his mom's privilege since he was a baby, but he wanted a story from me. It was an amazing reaction to a few simple comments. It was a good feeling to see him react that way.

I didn't have as much luck with my wife. Is it possible that a person's bucket can be so filled with holes that you can't get anything to go in?

I tried to fill her bucket, just like you said, but nothing worked. I tried a few times for a couple of days and gave up. The only thing that she seemed to notice was that our son asked me to read him a story. Any suggestions?

I'm also working on Jerry, the other assignment you gave me. I'll have a report for our next class.

From: Coach
Reply-To: Coach@consultingcompany.com
To: <Scott@acompany.com
Subject: The News

Thanks for your message. I'm glad to hear about your son. A six-year-old can be a lot of fun. I'm never surprised at how quickly some people react to their bucket being filled. Your son must be like that, just a little positive effort, and you saw a major gain. Keep it up. Remember, though, he will need regular deposits for quite some time to compensate for what he may have missed from you in the past six years.

I'm also not surprised at your wife's reaction. Depending on how long the two of you have had problems, it may take some time to repair the damage. Be honest, truthful, and forthright. Don't embellish or diminish. Look for opportunities to put something in her bucket, and don't be upset if you don't see a reaction like you did with your son. The important thing is to try, especially reinforcing what you like and appreciate about her. Positive feedback is a powerful tool, it can heal serious wounds, but in some situations it may take time.

Keep working with Jerry. I'll look forward to your report at our next session.

Next Classroom Session

A week later the group assembled in the company's meeting room for their next session with the coach. Scott's boss was pleased that everyone seemed interested in being there and learning how to deal more effectively with others. He was watching the group's reaction to this process carefully, because these managers could be fairly critical of any outside program that they felt was a waste of time. He assumed this was the result of a companywide downsizing a couple of years earlier where only the "best and brightest" had survived the layoffs. The current group of managers were overachievers who often worked, if anything, too much and too hard. That's why they could be critical of anything that they felt wasted their time. So he was pleased to see that everyone was there before the scheduled start time ready to see what would come next.

"In our last session," the coach began, "we heard about how the feedback we receive goes into our feedback bucket. Our teams explained to us about the holes in the bottom, how they get there and a few ways to plug them up. I hope you've all had a chance to think about what we discussed. Today we're going to look at the four types of interpersonal feedback."

The coach walked to a whiteboard and removed a piece of paper that had been taped to the board. Now exposed was a large circular model that was constructed of a laminated material. The managers could see representations of the four types of feedback. In the middle of the model was an illustration of a feedback bucket. The coach continued, "The feedback bucket is placed in the middle of the model, because all feedback, whether positive or negative, flows into the bucket. Mentally healthy people obviously prefer positive feedback, but when a bucket is empty, people will even accept negative feedback. That's because the emotional pain of an empty bucket is greater than the pain of receiving negative feedback."

In succession, she pointed at the words around the perimeter of the model as she explained, "The four types of interpersonal feedback are supportive, corrective, insignificant, and abusive. We will have an opportunity in later sessions to discuss each type and demonstrate the important ones, but let me introduce them briefly to you now."

Pointing at *SUPPORTIVE FEEDBACK*, she continued, "The

Figure 4-1. Four-types-of-feedback model.

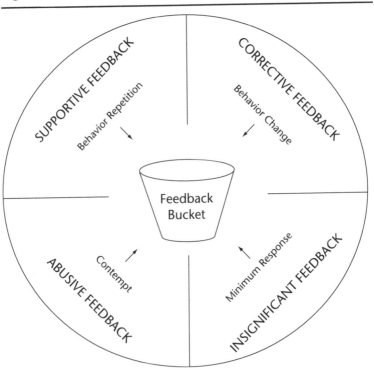

primary purpose of supportive feedback is to reinforce a behavior you want repeated. In other words, when someone exhibits a behavior that you like or you would like repeated, the single most important thing you can do is to make a strong, supportive deposit in that person's feedback bucket reinforcing that specific behavior. If you don't, because you're too busy or you don't think it's necessary, you may not see that behavior repeated."

Next she pointed at *CORRECTIVE FEEDBACK* and continued, "The purpose of corrective feedback is to change a behavior. Simply stated, if a person's behavior needs to be changed, the best chance of making that happen is to give corrective feedback. The problem is that most people don't know how to give corrective feedback—they mistake abusive feedback for corrective feedback. As you'll see in a later session, without training and practice, most people are ineffective in giving corrective feedback—quite frankly, it can be a challenging conversation."

While pointing at *INSIGNIFICANT FEEDBACK*, she said, "Feedback that has little importance or meaning, or carries little impact is called insignificant—because compared to the other types, it really is insignificant. Feedback that is so vague or general that the person receiving it could be unsure of its purpose is likely insignificant feedback. Too many of us use insignificant feedback believing it will have a huge positive effect. Actually, it doesn't. It brings only a minimal response from the other person."

Pointing at *ABUSIVE FEEDBACK*, she added, "All other types of feedback fall into the fourth category, called abusive feedback." The coach paused a few seconds to look around the room. After the point had sunk in, she continued. "So in other words, the feedback you give other people in your interpersonal relationships is either supportive, corrective, insignificant, or abusive. And the type of feedback you choose determines the response you will get."

Several people in the room glanced at each other and then back to the coach. She let the silence linger a while longer so the impact of the moment would reinforce what she obviously believed was an important point in her presentation. Most of the managers were thinking that if what she had said was true, then they must be guilty of giving abusive feedback themselves. That thought did not sit well with a couple of the people in the room.

After it seemed that no one was willing to break the silence, one of the managers raised his hand. "So you're saying that when I get upset at someone and tell him or her to 'shape up or ship out,' that I'm actually abusing that person?"

The coach took a couple of steps in his direction and asked, "When you tell someone to 'shape up or ship out,' are you supporting a behavior you want repeated, or are you trying to correct a specific behavior you want changed?"

The manager, realizing that he may have put his foot in his mouth, continued more carefully. "Well, I would hope that I was trying to correct something that wasn't working. That's why I would say, well actually I have said, to be honest, you've got to change or you'll force me to make a tough decision."

"It sounds like in that situation you're trying to change behavior with corrective feedback."

"Yeah, I guess I am."

"So telling someone to 'do it my way or you'll be on the highway' is an attempt to correct a behavior?"

"But sometimes the only thing left, after you've tried everything else, is to lay down a gauntlet. Isn't it?"

The coach looked at the class and said, "It might surprise some of you to hear me agree with that statement, provided you have, in fact, tried everything else. It's necessary, when the situation warrants it, to *draw a line in the sand*. If you don't, you can pay serious consequences later. But I'd like to reserve the discussion on drawing lines in the sand for another session."

A Bucket Shot Full of Holes

The coach turned to Scott and asked, "Scott, you told us about one of your employees. I believe your assessment was something like you 'had shot some holes in his bucket.' So I gave you an assignment to make a special effort to fill his bucket. Why don't you tell us what happened and how things are going?"

Scott's level of confidence with the group had increased to the point where he felt very comfortable explaining his problems with Jerry. A few weeks earlier he would have been embarrassed to discuss his failure with a key employee. But now that he had a better grasp of the situation, he was willing to be open and honest.

Scott said, "I think all of you know Jerry. He's one of my key account reps and I guess he's worked for us for what, six or seven years, something like that. For a long time he was my best worker and a top producer. His sales were high, profits high, virtually no customer problems. He wrote the book on how to keep his key accounts happy. The perfect employee!"

Scott became a little more reflective and continued, "Yeah, the perfect employee. The problem was how I *dealt* with the perfect employee. The better he became, the more I ignored him. At the time it seemed like a good idea to get out of his way and give him the freedom I thought he wanted. I created a problem by leaving him alone because I actually cut off what he needed most—feedback.

"Then, a little less than a year ago things began to change with Jerry's performance. It didn't happen overnight. It was fairly gradual, but over a number of months his numbers went downhill. But you've got to understand that I had a couple of other employees who had serious performance problems, so I spent most of my time working with them, because I thought that was the best use of my time. It just seemed that Jerry didn't need much of my time, so I didn't give it to him."

"Tell us more about Jerry's behavior during the time when his performance declined."

"Nothing happened at first. But now that I think about it, there were several times that he came to see me and asked some fairly simple questions about a customer account. There's no doubt in my mind that he already knew the answers. And he did that a few times during those months. I don't remember exactly what I said to him, but I'm sure that I must have blown him off on those occasions."

"And now that you've learned the importance of feedback, what was he really asking with those questions?"

"I don't think his questions were related to customers at all. I think he was saying, 'Pay attention to me. I'm being ignored.' To use a phrase I've learned in these classes, Jerry was saying 'Fill my bucket!' "

The coach looked from Scott to the class and said, "We've just learned an important principle. Let's clarify to make sure we're all on the same page. In this example, what were the warning signs that Scott wishes he had recognized with Jerry?"

"Watch out for people whose questions aren't really questions—they could actually be pleas for attention," one of the managers replied.

Another manager added, "But there's something else that we shouldn't forget. If you don't balance your feedback among your employees, you could end up with someone like Jerry."

"I like both of those comments," the coach said; then she turned back to Scott. "Now back to Jerry. Scott, did these warning signals from Jerry occur before, during, or after you denied him feedback?"

"Before, during, or after . . . I'm not sure, but my best guess is all three, because I've never really given him enough. I think his pleas for help began when his bucket got a little low, and have continued until recently, when I began paying more attention to him."

"We'll get to what's been going on the last couple of weeks in a minute. First, I'd like to make sure we understand the process. When did Jerry's performance drop off—how soon after your feedback stopped?"

"Oh, maybe a few weeks or a month or two, no more than that," Scott responded.

The coach smiled and continued, "Thanks for your assessment, Scott. It's not easy to bare your soul the way you have for us. Now that we understand what most likely caused the problem, what have you done in the past couple of weeks to improve the situation?"

"Let me say one thing first. It was in our first couple of sessions that the reality of what happened struck me. I think at first

I was probably in denial. I was thinking that there was no way that I could be responsible for what was obviously someone else's production problem. But then the more we talked about how important feedback is to us, the more my involvement in the cause of the problem became apparent."

"Good insight, Scott. How about giving us a progress report."

"I've tried to spend a few minutes each day with Jerry. Some days it's tough with my schedule. But I'm getting at least five to ten minutes each day, and a couple of times up to, say, twenty minutes."

"So far, what has been his reaction?" the coach wanted to know.

All eyes in the room were on Scott. The managers were clearly interested in the story about Jerry. Scott continued, "I think his first reaction was that I was doing it to catch him making a mistake so I could fire him. With my abrupt change in style, he assumed the worst."

"How much of his assumption that your motives were less than honorable might be related to his distrust of your relationship?"

"Probably all of it," Scott admitted.

"So when feedback is denied or withheld in a relationship, what happens to interpersonal trust?"

"From what I've seen, it probably disappears."

"I agree. So how's it going now?" the coach continued.

"It took a while, but he seems to have opened up a bit in the last week or so."

The coach walked to the whiteboard and printed *Trust* on the right side of the board. Then she turned to the class and asked, "Let's pursue what we've just learned. What's necessary in a relationship before one person can trust another person? In other words, what happens in a relationship that causes trust to develop?"

There was silence in the room while the managers contemplated the answer. It was obviously not an easy question. A woman finally broke the silence and replied, "Before two people can trust each other, don't they first have to know or understand each other, at least to some extent?"

The coach smiled and responded, "Absolutely! That is true. Understanding must come first."

Then she went to the middle of the whiteboard and printed *Understanding*. Now there was a space on the board to the left of *Understanding*, and another space between *Understanding* and *Trust*. The coach continued, "Understanding does precede trust. But, something comes before understanding, and something else occurs between understanding and trust. This is a four-step process that we really need to understand in order to develop effective relationships. So what two elements of this process are missing?"

Now there was an eerie dead silence in the room. The expressions on the managers' faces indicated that they were stumped.

After what seemed like a never-ending silence, the coach added, "Most of you have probably never considered what causes trust between you and your employees. We all want it. We believe things would work better with it. At times we even depend on it. The CEO in the manufacturing company I told you about knew he didn't have it. In fact, he could sense that he didn't have it, but didn't know why."

The coach looked back at the whiteboard and said, "So something happens prior to understanding. What would that be?"

"People have to talk first, don't they?" The same woman replied, with an anxious look on her face.

The coach turned to the whiteboard and printed *Communication* to the left of *Understanding*. Then she said, "Before we can understand where other people are coming from, there must first be some element of communication. People have to relate to each other. Without communicating effectively, there won't be much understanding, and ultimately little or no trust."

The coach pointed to the one remaining space between *Un-*

Figure 4-2. Developing respect and trust.

Communication = Understanding = Respect = Trust

derstanding and *Trust* and continued, "So now we are only miss-ing one of the four elements. Something happens in a relationship after we gain understanding, but prior to the development of real trust. Before I trust you, I most likely will . . ."

The coach stopped in midsentence and waited for an answer.

The same manager blurted out, "Respect! I don't trust some-one until I respect him!"

The coach smiled as she turned to the whiteboard and filled in the missing element with *Respect*.

Then the coach added three equal signs to complete the model she had drawn on the board. Turning back to the managers she summarized what they had created. "I said earlier that it took several months for the CEO in the manufacturing company to gain the trust of his employees. That's because before his employ-ees could trust him they had to first respect him. And before they could respect him they had to first understand him. And before they could understand him as their leader, he had to communi-cate effectively with them. So the process began with effective communication and ended with increased levels of trust in the factory."

The coach took a couple of steps from the whiteboard toward the managers and said, "Giving feedback effectively is one of the most powerful techniques of communication. When we improve our feedback skills, we begin the process of building understand-ing, respect, and finally trust in a relationship. That's how power-ful these concepts are."

Three Steps for Scott

The coach took a close look at Scott, and sensing that he might be ready to move to a higher level, asked, "Scott, regarding Jerry, what do you think you ought to do next to build more trust in your relationship?"

"Keep giving feedback, I guess." Scott glanced around the room. The looks on the faces of a couple of the managers seemed to be saying that there was something else that he had missed. So he asked, "Or is there something else you think I should do?"

"You could maintain the increase in supportive feedback, but I believe Jerry deserves to know how you feel about what happened. You've admitted to us that you should have handled the situation differently. He clearly deserves to know what you plan to do in the future. If what I'm saying is correct, what could you do to move the improvement to the next level?"

Scott paused, unsure of what direction she might be going. Before he could fumble his way through an answer, Scott's boss interjected, "I'm not sure where you're going with that question, but it occurs to me that Jerry might deserve an apology."

The coach raised her eyebrows and asked, "An apology . . . what do you think, Scott?"

"Wow! That would be a bit much. I'd have to think about that." Scott looked down at his class notes and started to write something, crossed it out, and shook his head. It was obvious that he was uncomfortable admitting his mistake to Jerry. Scott had always taken a great deal of pride in himself, but a thought crossed his mind of a time a few years ago when his wife had told him that his pride was getting in the way of him admitting his mistakes. He wondered if that was the issue now.

The coach could see that Scott was uncertain, so she proceeded more carefully. "You might consider a three-step process to improve your situation with Jerry. You've already stopped the critical feedback and stepped up your supportive feedback. Those are the first two steps. What do you suppose is the third step?"

"I'll bet you're going to say an apology."

"Actually, that is the third step, but it's up to you. Sometimes the best way to forge a new beginning is to face up to what's happened in the past and then move forward with better behaviors. An apology might help. It's your decision. Think about it."

"I'm not saying it isn't a good idea. It's a good suggestion. I've just got to give it some thought. That's all."

"Fair enough, we'll settle for that."

There was a part of Scott that enjoyed being the focus of attention in the class, and there was another part of him that was uncomfortable with the attention. He wasn't a person who naturally liked being in the spotlight, particularly for extended periods of time, yet he enjoyed being recognized for his accomplishments, especially when he felt he deserved the recognition. And he was willing to accept the consequences of the few times in his career when he had made blunders. Nonetheless, as he left the meeting room he was a little confused about what to do next with Jerry.

Before he got back to his office to begin sorting out the day's challenges, his decision became clear as a fellow class member said, "I can't wait to see how your meeting with Jerry goes. Good luck." Scott knew then what he had to do.

Blinding Flash of the Obvious (BFO) & Food Always Works (FAW)

The last meeting with the coach and the managers had ended with a challenge. It was obvious that every manager attending was interested in Scott's story about Jerry. Most of the managers knew Jerry, or at least they were familiar with who he was in the organization, so they could relate to the problem on both a personal and a professional level. And, although they wouldn't admit it in public, several of the managers had made mistakes similar to Scott's, and that drew them into following the progress of the situation.

Scott received encouragement from a few of his closest friends among the group of managers during the days that followed. One manager sent him an e-mail expressing her admiration for Scott admitting his mistake in an open setting. She said, "I'm not sure I could have been so open in a group that is so highly competitive.

We aren't used to someone in our group exposing his shortcomings. So I admire your courage in being so honest."

Scott sent a thank-you reply that included, "You're right. We are a competitive bunch, but that isn't all bad. Our competitiveness has made us a strong company. But I feel bad about Jerry because I believe that I'm responsible for one of our best employees losing his focus and drive. That's why I think it's necessary for me to use the information we're learning in the training classes as soon as possible so I can help reverse Jerry's direction. Based on what I've seen so far, it's looking good. Thanks for your encouragement."

Manager in the Hallway

A manager with whom Scott worked quite closely was particularly impressed with the story about Jerry. On the day following the last meeting he stopped Scott in a hallway and asked, "Didn't you see the problem with Jerry coming, or did it just sneak up on you?"

Scott wasn't sure how to take the question. Did he mean, "Were you so blind that you couldn't see what was happening? Didn't you know that if you shut someone out he might react badly?" Or did he mean, "Did Jerry's performance erode gradually over time, or did it drop overnight?" Scott was unsure what the question meant, and his first thought was that if he'd been asked that question a month earlier, he might have snapped back at a close colleague. Now he realized that for some time he had been wound tight as a spring due to all the pressures in his life, both at work and at home.

Scott assumed the best of intentions and responded, "I know I should have seen it coming. And, I can't believe that I didn't see the connection between giving Jerry appropriate feedback and his performance problems. Once it started, I just focused on what he was doing wrong and what he wasn't getting done. And the more

I did that, the more he seemed to go downhill, which caused me to focus even more on the negative. It was a vicious downward cycle: The more I focused on the negative, the more his performance went downhill, and so the more I seemed to focus on the negative. So, no, I guess I didn't see it coming."

The friend was afraid that he may have pushed Scott too far, so he put his hand on Scott's shoulder and said, "Hey, I hope you don't think I'm trying to put you down. It's not that at all. The truth is, I did the same thing. I've had the same problem, but it wasn't my best employee; it was my wife. Actually, to be accurate, my ex-wife."

The manager looked down the hall for a second as if searching for a way out of the conversation. Hesitantly, he turned back to Scott, unable to speak. Seeing the pain on his friend's face, Scott said, "I was aware that you had problems at home, but I guess I didn't know what really happened."

The manager paused briefly and was able to continue, "Some of the things we've talked about in the last few weeks have hit me pretty hard. What you just said about focusing on the negative—that's what I did to my ex. It's really hard for me to admit, but the truth is, for fourteen years I focused on what I thought she was doing wrong. I pointed out anything I didn't like, and I did it in an abusive way. I completely failed to recognize or appreciate all the things she did for our son and me. It was that negative focus thing—just like you said. And now I can see that my focus on negative feedback caused the downward spiral that led to our divorce. Two marriage counselors tried to tell me what I was doing, but I couldn't see it. My ex tried to tell me what I was doing, but I refused to see it. I've been wondering lately if maybe I didn't want to see what was going on. So that's why what you're doing with Jerry is so important to me. I've got a personal stake in it. I guess I've lived it before, only at a different level."

Scott could see the hurt in his friend's face. It was clear that he was still suffering great pain from the divorce. And now Scott understood that this colleague wanted him to succeed not only for Jerry's sake, but also for another more personal reason. Scott confided, "I haven't been the best manager, husband, or father, for that matter. I've made the same mistakes at work and at home. I'm sorry about what happened to you. I know you've got a son about ten isn't he? How is he doing?"

"He's almost twelve now, but he gets bounced back and forth from my place to his mother's. And now she remarried her old high school boyfriend, so he's got a stepdad. It's not a good way to raise a son. I don't think this mess would have happened if I had stopped the negative focus and given more positive feedback to my wife. I mean my ex-wife."

Now Scott could tell the extent of the pain in his friend's life. "I'm sorry. Maybe what we've learned about feedback can help a little."

"I'm afraid it's too late to fix the problems with my ex, but I've got to work on my son. I don't want to lose him, too."

Scott wondered if his friend was just a few years ahead of where he could be if he didn't change things at home. The pain on his friend's face told Scott that the path of divorce wasn't something he wanted to follow.

The conversation ended with each of them offering encouragement to the other. But Scott couldn't forget the look on his friend's face as he described what he believed had caused his divorce. It reminded Scott of something a former boss had said when Scott had finally seen something that had been staring him in the face for some time but he hadn't seen it. His boss had called it a blinding flash of the obvious, or BFO. That's what had just happened to his friend, a BFO. In fact, that's what had happened to Scott in the last meeting.

The Third Step

The next day Scott was looking for Jerry through a growing crowd. "Hey, Jerry, over here." Scott waved Jerry over to the table he was saving. He had asked Jerry to meet him for lunch at a diner where he had taken clients before. The diner was a popular eating spot for the business crowd and specialized in quick service and great food. He had saved a table that he thought would afford them a little privacy for the conversation he needed to have. At 11:30, the diner was just beginning to pick up its lunch business. "Thanks for meeting me, Jerry. I wanted to get away from the commotion and all the interruptions at the office, so I thought a lunch would work."

On the outside Jerry nodded his agreement, but on the inside he was apprehensive. Scott had never invited him to lunch before. He knew Scott took clients to lunch, but he had never been included. He saw Scott as professional and cordial, but clearly not social with employees. He was nervous about the meeting, because going to lunch was not like the old Scott. A few months ago he was concerned that Scott might fire him. But there had been a noticeable change in Scott's treatment of his employees in the past few weeks. So he wasn't sure which Scott would show up to lunch: the old Scott, who seemed to thrive on being critical over the least of mistakes, or the new Scott, who seemed to take a sincere interest in his employees.

"Have you eaten here before?" Scott asked. "It's pretty good."

"Didn't even know this place was here, but it's sure crowded for this early in the day," Jerry replied.

In a supervisory course Scott had attended a couple of years earlier, the instructor used a phrase that had stuck in his mind: "Food always works!" He used the acronym FAW as a reminder that when you have an important discussion and you need to set the person at ease, food always works. Food or something to munch on, he said, can create an informal setting where people are more likely to listen, and be less defensive. That's why Scott had staged this discussion at the diner, in hopes that food would be his ally and set Jerry at ease.

Scott had played out this conversation several times in his

mind, but he was unsure where to begin. In the past few weeks he had consciously tried to eliminate the criticism and reinforce the positive with Jerry. And so far it seemed to be making a difference. However, this was the conversation where he needed to apologize for what he had done and forge a better working relationship.

He couldn't think of any other way to begin, so after they placed their orders he launched off with, "Jerry, I need to talk with you about something that is very important to me. I haven't been a very effective supervisor for you and the other people in our division. I've been overly critical and I haven't been available when you needed me. I know there have been times when you needed my help and I've brushed you off. But I want you to know that I realize what I've done and I'm trying hard to be a better leader."

Jerry was looking down at the menu he was still holding in his hands. He put it down, suddenly realizing the server had already taken their order. He slid the menu in a slot at the back of the table but found it difficult to look Scott in the eye, not knowing what to say, but fully agreeing with what Scott had just said. He paused and replied, "That would be helpful."

There was an uncomfortable silence until Scott said, "Tell me what you've been thinking these past few months."

Jerry had been thinking a lot lately, but he didn't know how much to say at this time. He shrugged his shoulders and replied, "I know I've let you down and I know my numbers have crashed. But I don't think the company has cut me any slack for things that I can't control."

Jerry had said that the *company* hadn't cut him any slack for things that he couldn't control, but Scott knew what Jerry really meant. Scott hadn't cut Jerry any slack. Sensing that this conversation could blow up in his face, Scott knew that he had to stay positive and keep Jerry talking. Using techniques he had learned years before, but hadn't used lately, Scott said, "Tell me what things are out of your control."

"Well, for one, every time we revamp our product line there is a lag in sales from the old products until the new line gets established and then sales pick up. I've seen it before. That's what we've got right now—sales are down because we discontinued some important products and replaced them with a new series of items. If we'll all be patient and not overreact, sales will bounce back. They always have before."

Earlier in his career Scott learned what a teacher called the Socratic listening technique, but he knew he hadn't used it for a long time. Realizing he needed to keep Jerry talking, he tried it now and said, "You think we've overreacted."

"Yeah, I do. We've got to be patient. The last time we did this it took about six months for sales to rebound. Now we're about six months past the changes we made, so if we don't panic, sales on the new line ought to kick in real soon and we'll be just fine. In fact, I can already see the light at the end of the tunnel."

"And if we're not patient?" Scott asked.

Wondering how far he dare push the subject, Jerry continued, "I think too much pressure put on account reps right now will only be passed on to our loyal customers. And if they don't like being pushed into buying the new line before they are ready, then we could be in a lot of trouble by the end of the year."

"How much trouble?" Scott asked.

"Hard to tell, but at least a loss of 20 percent in that product category."

Scott had just had another BFO. Jerry was right. He had a better grasp of what was going on than Scott or any of his colleagues. This was good information.

But Scott knew he had to broach the reason for the lunch. "That's good insight, Jerry. I think you've got some really good points. We need to continue this conversation tomorrow. Let me get back to what I was saying a minute ago. How about the pressure I've been putting on you this past year?"

Jerry paused, still not sure how far to go. He seemed to be

dealing with the new Scott, but he wasn't sure. So he responded, "It's been real intense."

"How has my intense pressure made you feel?"

"You want the answer I should give, or do you want the truth?" Jerry visibly flinched at his own words. He had promised himself as he entered the diner that he was going to control what he said so he wouldn't upset Scott. Did he just break his promise? He wasn't sure.

"Jerry, I need the truth, please. It's important to me that you tell me exactly what you've been thinking and how you're feeling."

"Well, I'm not happy, if that's what you want to hear."

Scott explained, "To be an effective leader I think it's more important to hear what I *need* to hear, instead of hearing only what I *want* to hear. I know I've been critical of your work performance. At times I think I've been sarcastic as well. And when I'm not critical or sarcastic I've probably been indifferent to what you needed from me."

There was an uneasy silence at the table. Their sandwiches fortunately arrived just then and neither of them said anything of substance while they began eating their lunch. After a minute or two Scott continued, "I'm sorry that I took out my frustrations on you. You need to know that for the past few years, you've been my go-to guy. When the chips were down I could always count on you to score for me. And when I needed you the most, with the product changes and all, I responded by doing exactly what I shouldn't have done. And for that I'm sorry. I hope you'll accept my apology."

Jerry looked up at Scott and put his fork down on his plate. After wiping his mouth with a napkin, he said, "I didn't think you cared how I felt."

"Jerry, I do care how you feel, in spite of how I've treated you. Tell me this—when was the last time you seriously considered leaving the company?"

Without a pause, Jerry said, "The last time? How about a few minutes ago while I was driving over here for lunch?" Jerry wished he had held his tongue. He feared now that he had overstepped the line.

"I was afraid that you had considered leaving. I'm sorry for not respecting your contributions to the company, particularly our division in the company. We need you, especially now that sales are about to blossom with the new line. I promise you that I'll control the criticism and sarcasm. I'll pay more attention to your needs, and we'll talk more. When your performance is good and you do things right, I'll tell you. And if there are problems, I'll let you know. But I'll do it in an appropriate way. Sound okay?"

Jerry had just heard exactly what he thought he'd never hear from Scott. He couldn't remember a time when Scott had given an apology, especially one that came from the heart. He also liked the part about hearing when he did things right. That was exactly what he wanted most from his boss. So he said, "Sound okay? It would be great."

They finished lunch talking about some ideas Jerry had about how to boost sales of the new product line. Scott once again turned to his supervisory training and took notes about the conversation so that Jerry would feel validated as he expressed his ideas.

On the way back to the office, Scott reflected on his lunch with Jerry. He could sense the value of applying the principles of feedback. He could visualize that he had made a substantial deposit in Jerry's feedback bucket. It felt good. Out loud he said to no one in particular, "It really feels good to fill a person's bucket and the BFO and FAW weren't so bad either!"

What to Reinforce

"Hi there, I hope it's okay to call you on the phone. Have you got a minute?" Scott didn't want to wait until the next training class, and e-mail was a little too impersonal for what he needed to discuss.

The coach leaned back in her chair and said, "No problem at all. I'm catching a plane in a while, but I've got some time. How are you doing with your assignments?"

"That's why I called. I did the three things you suggested with Jerry. As you heard, I cut out the negative feedback. You called it abusive feedback, actually. I stepped up the positive, or supportive, feedback by trying to catch him doing the right things. And I took him to lunch two weeks ago and apologized for what I've been doing the past few months."

"Apologizing for something like that isn't easy. Many people I deal with in the business community have too much pride to admit their mistakes. How did that meeting go?"

"I told him how much he had contributed to the company for several years. I tried to be as specific as I could. I don't know if this was a good idea or not, but I told him that I had made a mistake in shutting him out while I was dealing with some other problems. I apologized for what I had done."

"And what was his response?"

"At first, he just sat there; I think he was a little stunned. He said that he knew he had let me down, and after a few minutes he began to open up."

"So you learned that abusive feedback oftentimes inhibits the free flow of information—sometimes vital information that you need to make good decisions."

"Yeah, that's right. He told me things that I would have never known if I hadn't apologized."

"So how has he reacted since your lunch meeting?"

"It's like someone waved a magic wand over his head. If you had told me that a person could make such a miraculous change in a couple of weeks just by filling his bucket, I'd have said you were nuts. To be honest, it's too good to be true. You should put this story in a book." Scott knew he was rambling on, but he was having a difficult time containing his excitement. The improvement with Jerry was merely the first of two pieces of good news that he had to share.

"Perhaps we *should* put it in a book some day. You sound excited. And you say his reaction was quite positive?"

"Wow, I'll say! Positive doesn't do justice to the change I've seen," Scott explained.

"That's great, Scott. I like how you followed through with those three steps. You should be excited about the improvement. But I'm curious, how exactly has Jerry changed?"

"I could be imagining what I've seen, but I'd swear that within just a couple of days of shutting down the criticism and sarcasm he began to change. It was so obvious that I'm actually embarrassed to admit how fast it happened."

"So he started improving almost immediately. Then what happened?"

"Well, as I said, I think there was an immediate improvement when I stopped the negative feedback. And then there was even more improvement as I stepped up the positive feedback. I think you predicted that, actually. Then I apologized and promised him that I would be more careful and honest in the future."

"That's a demonstration of good character, Scott."

"I know it's important to face up to your responsibilities. So I told Jerry what I had done and that I was sorry. He opened up immediately and told me some things about our product line that nobody else had considered. Like I said, Jerry has an incredible handle on our business and our customers." Scott had calmed down somewhat but was obviously still excited.

The coach had a smile on her face, but Scott couldn't tell that over the phone. She said, "There's a sound business principle that the person closest to the problem is likely to have the best and the most practical solution. I think you just proved that principle true. How are your other projects coming?"

It took Scott a second to figure out what other projects she was referring to. But then he knew. "You mean my feedback problems at home. I've got good news and some not-so-good news."

"What happened?"

"Let me tell you the good news. It's about my wife. You remember that before we started the classes at work that I had been just as critical of her as I had been of Jerry. I had a focus problem with my wife, just like I did with Jerry. When I looked for things I didn't like, I found them. And the more I found, the more I could see."

"When you focus on the negative, you can get in a downward spiral," the coach added.

"I heard someone else say the same thing and that's what happened to me. The more I did it, the more things I found to criticize. But I've really been working hard at not just controlling my focus problem, but also at filling her bucket every chance I get."

"I recall you said that for the first few weeks there wasn't much reaction from her."

"Not really. But very slowly she has begun to include me in her life. It's not much, but it's a good start. I have you to thank for what I hope is a new beginning for us."

Three Steps at Home

"No thanks are necessary, but they are certainly appreciated. My role is to ask tough questions. You have the difficult part. You have to put the ideas into action. Speaking of tough questions, what else do you need to do regarding your wife?"

"What else? Well, there are so many things I need to do to make things work. Which one are you thinking about?"

"There is something that you did with Jerry that I think would be appropriate with your wife."

"You're referring to an apology, aren't you?"

"What do you think about using the same three steps on your wife that you used with Jerry?"

Scott wasn't sure if another apology would be easier, or more difficult. The painful image of his colleague in the hallway flashed in his mind. His friend wished he could turn back the calendar several years and do things differently. If that were possible, perhaps he could have saved his marriage, but now it was too late. For Scott, giving an apology might be difficult, but if it would help, he was willing to try. He had already used the first two steps: He had stopped the critical feedback and he had increased the supportive feedback. The only step left was an apology. While these thoughts passed through his mind, the coach could sense by the silence on the phone line that Scott was struggling with something—perhaps something else. Not wanting to lose this opportunity, the coach asked, "You're struggling with something. What is it?"

"I know I should apologize, so I'll do it. But I've got to make sure it's the right time."

Through her intuition, the coach pushed a little more. "I sense there is something else. What else is bothering you?"

Scott paused and started to move the telephone handset away from his mouth but then moved it back and began. "In the last couple of months I've been able to make things a little better with my wife, a lot better with my son, and Jerry. But my daughter won't give me the time of day. I've tried everything I know, everything you've taught me, but nothing seems to work. She is distant and doesn't seem to respond to me in any way. She's growing up before my eyes and I feel like a detached witness. I'm afraid that if I can't fix my relationship with her really soon, one day I'll look up and she'll be gone from my life forever."

"So there's no focus problem, and you're being careful with your feedback?"

"I've done everything I can. I only give her supportive feedback. I cut out the critical feedback, but it doesn't seem to work. It's like she's holding a grudge against me. And with such good results on my other projects, as you call them, I'm really concerned. I want things to be better with my daughter, too."

"Scott, give me an example of the type of feedback you've been giving her."

"This morning as she was leaving to catch the school bus I told her that she looked nice. And last night while she was doing her homework, I told her how smart I think she is. You know, comments like that."

"And so far what's been her reaction to what you've said?"

"Nothing. She doesn't do anything. And I almost see a little contempt on her face. I guess it's her reaction that has me so concerned."

The Abused Woman

"Perhaps I can answer your question with an experience I had a few years ago. A woman attended a presentation I did for a company where I discussed feedback. When the session was over this woman sat frozen in her chair while everyone else left the room. She had a perplexed look on her face. After I gathered up my materials, I walked over and said, 'You seem puzzled about something.' But she didn't respond. She didn't say anything. So I assumed that I had either offended her in some way, or something else was bothering her.

"I waited a short while and then began to walk out of the room when she said, 'I just figured it out.'

"I stopped and asked, 'What did you figure out?'

"She said, 'I just figured out what he did to me.'

"I didn't have a clue what she was saying, so I said, 'Someone did something to you?'

"It took her a few minutes to open up, but when she did I heard a story that was almost too incredibly horrifying to believe. She said that she had no recollection of her father ever calling her by her given name. She had never heard him verbalize her name. He only referred to her as 'Dumb Sh__.' He would say, 'Hey, Dumb Sh__, get over here.' Or, 'Hey, Dumb Sh__, do this,' or 'do that.'

"There was so much abusive feedback in this woman's childhood, mostly from her father, that she actually believed she was intellectually inferior to other people. Her belief that she was *dumb* crossed over into all other aspects of her life. As a result, she grew up with massive feelings of intellectual inferiority, which led to social insecurity. She told me how her negative feelings about herself had impacted her in virtually every way. The effects of the abuse were apparent to me by the way she walked, how she dressed, and how she took care of herself.

"But somewhere in that class on feedback she began to understand that if you hear something repeated often enough as feedback, you can believe it to be true, whether it is or not. Because of her father's power position in the family, she *believed* his abusive feedback. I could tell the extent of her pain when she asked me,

'Do you know what it's like to have your father call you "Dumb Sh__" in front of your friends?'"

Scott was disturbed by the story, because he wasn't sure what it had to do with him. He asked, "You're not saying that I've done that to my daughter?"

"No, no, Scott. I'm not saying that at all. But there is a good principle about feedback that we can learn from the story, and I'd like you to consider it regarding the feedback you give to your daughter. Looking at your relationship with your daughter, there are three basic things you could reinforce with feedback. The first is how she looks, or her appearance. The second is what she does, or her behavior. And the third is who she is, or the person inside the outward appearance. If you use your position power as her father and mostly reinforce how she looks, she grows up to believe that she must *look good* in order to be accepted, especially by men. And that obviously becomes more difficult as she grows older. If you mostly reinforce what she does, she grows up to believe that she must *do things* in order to be accepted. So she can become a *people pleaser*. Both of those reinforcements are good, if they are done in realistic proportion to the third type of feedback, which is who she is as a person. In other words, it is important for you to tell your daughter that she is pretty and that she does good things. But it's equally important for you to tell her that you love and accept her as a person. She must believe that the person inside her is a good person who has value to herself and others."

Scott added, "So what her father did by calling her 'Dumb Sh__' was to attack who she was as a person—the exact thing he should have been reinforcing with positive comments."

"That's right, Scott. With your daughter, it's important that she be convinced that you like how she looks, that how she behaves makes you happy, *and* that you are proud of the person she is inside. All three are important types of reinforcing feedback that you need to provide."

The coach paused and then asked, "Which of these three

types have you been reinforcing these past few weeks with your daughter?"

"It's been what she does, her behavior, and a little of how she looks. But I don't think I've done anything in the third category at all."

"So what changes do you need to make in the type of reinforcing feedback you give your daughter in the next few weeks?"

"I need to balance the three types of reinforcement."

"That's right. Be sure to make your comments sincere. Don't give her untrue comments just to impress her. What you say, especially to a person who has been denied real feedback, must come from the heart. Do that and let's see what happens."

Scott didn't want to lose the moment, so he asked, "If those are the things I do for my daughter, how about my son? What does he need?"

"Supportive reinforcement to boys and girls is pretty much the same. A variation in feedback between boys and girls has more to do with their interests and aptitudes than it does their gender. For example, many parents assume that boys need to excel at sports and in the classroom, so they direct a lot of their feedback on sports and grades. As a result, many boys grow up believing it's what you *do* in life that makes you a good person. Doing good things isn't bad; it's just that a boy needs to grow up knowing that acceptance and significance in life come as much from *who* you are as a person, as what you can do with a baseball bat or on a math test. Don't forget—if your daughter has an interest in sports, it's important to give her feedback in that area. When the chips are down and the pressure is on, it's our character that makes us the person we really are. Developing good behavior from your children is nice, but what you really want to do is help them develop sound character. That will help them throughout their lives, especially when they must make decisions on their own."

"That's a lot to take in at once," Scott said. "I like what you've said. I think I understand what I need to do with my son and daughter to help them develop their character, but besides the apology, what do I do for my wife? Are there some things I should be doing for her?"

"That's a good question. Why don't you consider giving her feedback in the same three areas we just discussed? Adults, who include employees, associates, and even bosses, can benefit from the same type of feedback that helps children. For now, I've got a plane to catch. So continue working on your assignments and keep me up-to-date."

"I'll do that. By the way, what happened to the woman whose father abused her?"

"There's an amazing ending to that story. And there will be some downtime on the plane; how about I tell you the ending in an e-mail?"

"Thanks a lot. I really appreciate your help. Have a nice flight."

"I'm planning on it."

Reinforcing the Positive

From: Coach
Reply-To: Coach@consultingcompany.com
To: <Scott@acompany.com
Subject: The Abused Woman

I had worked with abused people before, but this was the first time I had seen someone who was severely abused as a child, yet functioned moderately well in society as an adult. She had been an eighteen-wheel long-haul truck driver before she worked for the company where I met her. She was tough looking, overweight, and did little to take care of herself. Yet, her boss described her as his hardest-working employee. That was why she kept her job, in spite of how she looked, and her rough demeanor.

Then I met her in the class I described and she discovered that her father's comments were a severe type of emotionally abusive feedback. She realized, I think for the first time, that her poor fit into mainstream society was her reaction to her father's systematic abuse. That's why she said, "I just figured it out," in the class that day.

I didn't know it at the time, but I learned later that many employees in that company had given this woman a nickname. Because of her rough appearance and her gruff demeanor, many people called her "the blooper." I witnessed, firsthand, how painful those comments were. After she opened up to me, she confessed that on numerous occasions the comments by her fellow employees had moved her to tears.

Her boss gave me permission to meet with her once a week for almost a year while I was in that company working on some other issues. At first we talked about the connection she had made between her father's abuse and her behavior and appearance. Then we moved on to what she would like out of life and where she would like to go. I was impressed that she actually had high aspirations in the business world, but deep down she knew that promotions were out of reach until she could look and behave more professionally. She was actually fairly realistic about her situation. But it was her desire to improve herself that enabled me to help her that year. Without her desire, any progress would have been minimal.

I discovered that she was a sensitive, caring person. She was honest, hardworking, loyal, and dedicated. Inside, she was an incredibly impressive person. The problem was that her outward appearance and demeanor held the inner person hostage.

So in my sessions with her I used the feedback principles that we've been discussing to reinforce who she was and what she stood for. And I gave her corrective feedback when it was appropriate. She loved supportive feedback because she had heard so little of it in her life, and to her credit she honestly tried to learn from the corrective feedback.

The first real progress we made was when she agreed that change was necessary for her to achieve her goals. She agreed that if she continued in the direction she was going, she could only end up in the same place she had already been. And she agreed that where she currently was wasn't where she wanted to be. It may seem like a small insight for most of us, but to her it was a major breakthrough. It's been a number of years ago that this happened, but my recollection is that it took three or four months to make that much progress.

Slowly, I began to notice small changes in her appearance. She lost weight, she took some interest in her hair, and her clothes were cleaner and had a less rumpled look. The changes were subtle, but they became more obvious as time went on. With each improvement I provided supportive feedback, while continuing to reinforce the good person she was inside. The more feedback I gave, the more she seemed to change.

About seven or eight months after our first session, the woman faced a serious personal problem. Her grandmother passed away and her mother told her that she had to wear a dress to the funeral. But the woman didn't own any dresses, let alone one that would be suitable for a funeral. She was clearly too embarrassed to accept her mother's help, so I met her at a shopping mall to help her pick out an outfit. We met after work one day and made some nice selections, and then on the way out of the store we stopped by the cosmetics counter where a factory sales representative asked if we would like to see some new products. We agreed.

The woman attended the funeral a few days later and we continued our weekly sessions. A couple of months after the funeral, an amazing thing happened in that company. The abused woman wore the funeral outfit to work. She used a little makeup and fixed her hair. I was in the building that day and I heard at least a dozen people say something like, "Have you seen how good 'the blooper' looks today?" Even with a personal victory this woman continued to suffer the stigma of her former image. Some of her employees were unwilling or unable to forget the past and accept the new person.

The changes in her had been a slow process that took a number of months. Supportive feedback helped her change the way she viewed herself; and then she could change the way she appeared to others.

In the weeks that followed, there were even more improvements in the woman's appearance. As we increased the supportive feedback she received, her appearance continued to improve. And as her appearance improved, so did her social behaviors. That's because feedback, appearance, and behavior are connected by the self-image we have of ourselves. The improvement in her self-esteem created an inner glow that radiated in the look on her face. There actually came a time in that company when heads turned as she walked into a room. While her appearance improved, so also did her joy and satisfaction at being a high-performing employee for that company. As I look back on the experience, it is clear that her father's abusive feedback of calling her "Dumb Sh__" had affected her in every aspect of her life. But when she chose to not let her past hold her back, and when several of us stepped up our use of supportive feedback, her entire life changed.

If there is a downside to the story it is that the woman was unable to overcome the negative reputation people had of her in that company. She later moved to another state, where I heard she had married and was doing really well in the business world. The last I heard was that she was on track to achieve the business goals she had set for herself.

The moral of the story about this abused woman is that supportive feedback has incredible healing effects. It can overcome great obstacles in a person's life. Also note how easily the woman adjusted to supportive feedback. Mentally healthy people seem to have a natural desire for positive feedback. That's because our brains are wired to prefer the positive over the negative. Don't ever forget that.

By the way, supportive feedback is the topic of our next training session. You'll have a head start on your colleagues. See you then.

The Next Training Session

A couple of days after the coach's e-mail to Scott, the group of managers assembled in the meeting room for their next session. Scott's boss had started each of the previous training sessions with a few comments or announcements. So when he wasn't there at the appointed time to begin, no one was quite sure what to do. One of the managers asked, "Should we begin without him, or wait?"

No one seemed to know, and when the only solution was to begin, the door to the meeting room flew open and the boss hurriedly entered. He placed a couple of folders on the table and said, "I'm sorry I'm late. There was something I had to take care of, and it couldn't wait until later."

The coach stood up and pointed toward the whiteboard, where she had hung the Four-Types-of-Feedback Model.

She began by saying, "I know you remember the four types of feedback: supportive, corrective, insignificant, and abusive. Mostly today we're going to focus on supportive feedback as a powerful tool in achieving behavior repetition, and in modifying and shaping behavior. It's been my experience that most people

Figure 7-1. Four-types-of-feedback model.

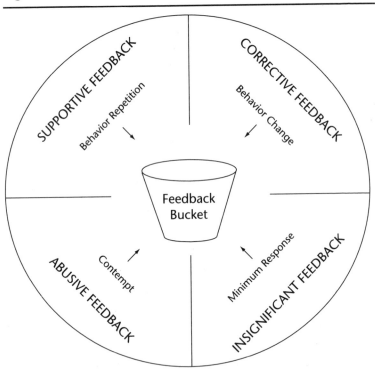

think they know all they need to about giving supportive feedback, but the truth is that most people are ineffective in giving it. Far too many people give *insignificant feedback* and believe it will have wonderful consequences. But that rarely, if ever, happens in most relationships. More on that later."

On the whiteboard the coach had printed three elements of supportive feedback.

The coach pointed to the list on the whiteboard and continued, "We are going to look at what supportive feedback is, what it isn't, and learn a highly effective method of giving supportive feedback both at work and at home. The technique will enable

Figure 7-2. Three elements of supportive feedback.

Supportive Feedback:
1. What it is
2. What it isn't
3. How to give it

you to give supportive feedback in most situations in the most powerful manner possible."

The coach appeared to shift gears as she looked from one person to the next. Finally, she said, "We briefly discussed the importance of supportive feedback a few weeks ago. We've all heard how Scott has used it to improve his relationship with Jerry, and that seems to be going well. And I know by the comments from several of you that supportive feedback has been on your minds a lot lately, too. Scott isn't the only manager with improved feedback skills."

The coach pulled a chair from the side of the room toward the middle where the tables were arranged. She sat down and said, "Before we get to the supportive feedback formula, I'd like a couple of you to share what you have done with feedback in the past month or so. Your examples can be from work or home. I'm not particular. But I would like you to focus on situations where you have specifically tried to use supportive feedback to reinforce or change behavior."

Looking to her left where Scott was seated, the coach said, "Scott, you've been a good example for all of us with your assignment with Jerry. And we appreciate that. But I'm curious what your colleagues have been doing, so let's excuse you from responding. For now, please hold your comments."

Then the coach glanced at Scott's boss. "And you've had a special assignment that we've kept under wraps for some time. Why don't you also hold off with your story until we hear from the others?"

The boss nodded his agreement but added, "My excuse for being late this morning is that I was on the phone getting an update on my own special assignment."

The coach looked back to the group and said, "Now that Scott and the boss are off the hook, let's hear from a couple of you. Who has consciously stepped up his or her use of supportive feedback and is willing to share what has happened?"

Two managers began speaking at once, but one yielded to the other, who said, "Let me say something before I tell my story. I've been in classes like this before. And quite frankly, they are all good in some way. What we're doing here isn't rocket science. We haven't covered anything that isn't plain common sense. It's the stuff we should already know, and we should have already been doing. But for some reason most of us haven't. That probably ought to be the subject of a discussion some time. How can something that is so important, but seems so simple, be so difficult to do, at least do on a fairly consistent basis?"

While the manager paused to collect her thoughts, the coach interjected, "Permit me to make a brief comment before you get to your example. You're right; feedback isn't rocket science. It's important, it's basic, and it's basically simple. The problem is that too many leaders and managers don't realize the importance of giving feedback, or filling those feedback buckets. I'm concerned that the feedback deficit in our society will only get worse. Thanks for your editorial. I couldn't agree more. How about an example?"

The manager quickly continued, "I've had a problem with my administrative assistant. We were clashing at least once a week, sometimes more often. If I wanted something done a certain way, she wanted it done a different way. If I wanted the header on a computer report centered, she said it looked better flush left. And this had been going on for I'll bet over a year. The problems were never earth-shattering, just annoying."

The manager opened a file folder on the table in front of her and pulled some papers that had been stapled together from the folder. As she held it up for everyone to see, she continued, "This is a computer report with the header centered, just the way I like it. Now I agree that getting the top few lines of a computer report printed in a particular way isn't a big deal, but the games we had been playing just illustrated the type of relationship that we had."

The manager put the report back in the folder and with a trace of a smile on her face continued. "How did I manage this great feat? I faced up to the fact that my style of feedback to this person had been largely negative and critical. When she was right, I ignored it. And when she was wrong, or when I *believed* she was wrong, I was quick to point it out. Does all this sound familiar?"

Chuckling, Scott asked, "Is your middle name Scott?"

As the laughter in the room subsided, the manager said, "I wish I could report that I had done some great psychological intervention with some fancy name, but all I did was the same thing Scott did. I cut out the critical comments and looked for things she did that I liked. I consciously look for an opportunity every day to give her some supportive feedback about some aspect of her job. I've been filling her bucket! Having it as a priority makes me pay closer attention to her work performance, which is good for me. I like the changes she has made. Hey, this stuff works!"

The coach thanked the manager for her report and asked, "Who else has a story to share?"

Another manager began, "My story isn't about an employee. It's about a vendor that I deal with almost every day. When these classes started, I tried using better feedback with the three prime contacts I have inside that company to see what would happen. In the past, when one of these contacts would come through for me in some way, I figured it was part of his job and he didn't deserve any comment. But I've made a conscientious effort to go out of my way to make sure that each person in this company who helps me gets recognized in some way. I've sent e-mails and made phone calls. Heck, I took a dozen donuts to a woman who got a special order out for me after she was scheduled to go home.

And just like what we've heard from the other examples, I'm getting better results lately from this company than I ever have in the past. The only thing I'm doing different is my feedback, so I know it's working for me, too."

"What type of feedback are you giving those people?" The coach asked.

"Nothing big. Just things like when I ask for some special consideration on a delivery, for example, and they come through on time, I make a special call or send an e-mail expressing my appreciation, which is, I guess, feedback."

"It is feedback and that's a great example. Thanks."

The Targets at SeaWorld

The coach had been seated at a table with the managers in the room as the stories had been shared. She stood and thanked the two managers for their comments and asked, "How many of you have been to a SeaWorld Adventure Park?"

Almost everyone in the room raised his or her hand, which caused the coach to comment, "I like this example because most people can relate to it. We can learn a lot from the trainers at SeaWorld, not just how to treat animals, but also how to treat people. What they do at SeaWorld isn't a secret. In their public shows they openly explain to the audience how positive reinforcement is used to change and model animal behavior. Those of you who haven't been to a SeaWorld park really need to go so that you can see for yourselves what I'm talking about."

The coach reached under a table where she had previously placed a rod about three feet long with a white knob stuck on one end that was about two inches in diameter. The knob seemed to have padding inside, which gave it a rounded look. The coach held the rod up for everyone to see and continued, "This is my miniature version of what the trainers at SeaWorld call a *target*. The actual targets the trainers use are very long so that they can reach out into the tanks with the animals. It's how the targets are used that impresses me."

The coach held the padded end of the target about a foot from the nose of one of the managers. Then she slowly moved the target closer until it touched his nose. With her other hand she handed him a small candy bar. The manager held the candy up and said, "I knew I liked this class."

The coach repeated the process a second time, once again giving the manager a candy bar. Looking at the class, she asked, "What do you think? Is this his favorite kind of fish?"

A third time she repeated the process, once again rewarding the manager with a candy bar.

Next she put the target about six inches from the manager's nose and said, "Let's assume that this candy is your favorite fish, and let's assume that you are hungry and would like more. If I place the target in front of you, like this, what would you most likely do?"

The manager leaned forward and touched the target with his nose and said, "That's not a tough question. Give me some more candy." Which she did.

The coach again looked at the manager and continued, "Let's assume you are still hungry and I place the target up here." She held the target as high as she could above the manager. "What would you do then?"

The manager stood on his chair so that he could touch the target and said, "That's what I would do. Now I'll take some more candy!" The strange sight of a manager standing on a chair caused the group a good laugh.

The coach put the target on the table and said, "Dolphins and killer whales may not have a human IQ, but patience, repetition, and reinforcement combined with the right type of reward can get an animal to jump out of the water and splash on the human fools who sit in the first few rows of the audience, called the 'splash zone.'

"SeaWorld is a great example for all of us because the trainers there have mastered the art of giving reinforcing feedback. It's not only their tradition, but it's also their trademark. The only sad part is that SeaWorld coaches and trains its animals far more effectively than most companies coach and train their employees."

Boys' Bedrooms

Later, after the group returned from a break, the coach said, "It's time now for us to get a report on a special project I gave your boss. I heard him say several months ago that he had two teenage sons whose bedrooms could be condemned by the health department. Those of you with teenagers can perhaps relate to his frustration." The coach looked at the boss and asked, "So why don't you explain what I asked you to do, and how it's been going?"

The boss stood up and said, "I think most of you know that I have two sons. One is seventeen and the other fourteen. Before I got here this morning, I called my wife for an up-to-the-minute report on their bedrooms. Both of their bedrooms have been a disaster for years, and nothing my wife or I have done has made much difference. I was given the assignment to watch for any spontaneous improvement in either of their bedrooms and then make a fuss about the improvement. It took quite a while to find some improvement, but I finally did with my fourteen-year-old. I went in one night after dinner and said, 'Wow, look at that. There aren't any clothes on your bed. And look over here; I think this corner is cleaner than it used to be. Hey, I really appreciate your efforts to clean your room.' Later that night, my wife told me to go see what was happening in his bedroom. He had a large garbage bag and was stuffing it with old pizza boxes and other things that would make the health department cringe. As our coach had schooled me, I praised him for the additional progress, which seemed to bring about even more cleaning. Now, he didn't make the room super presentable, by any means, but he did make more progress than I've seen in years."

The boss glanced at the coach, back to the managers and continued, "So the fourteen-year-old's room is much better, and the seventeen-year-old has made a little progress. What I've learned is that the secret to getting your children to clean their bedrooms is to praise the positive and be very careful about dwelling on the negative. I think criticism was one of the primary causes of our problem. I think what I have witnessed in my sons' bedrooms is a great model of what we need to do with our employees, and with each other for that matter. We need to dwell more on the positive, and be careful about the negative. And that's the report on my assignment."

Supportive Feedback Formula

The coach moved her chair in front of the boss and sat down. She looked directly at him and said, "Several weeks ago I asked you to take on a special project for me. I heard you describe your sons' bedrooms and knew you were frustrated. So I asked you to use supportive feedback at the first sign of any spontaneous improvement, no matter how small. You agreed to the assignment and came back today with really good results. Because of your feedback, you now have the opportunity to continue improving your relationship with your boys so that you can work on other issues. I want you to know how impressed I am with what you did, because not every executive I've dealt with would have done as well as you have. Thanks again."

The group of managers knew that what the coach had just done with their boss was unique. The way it had been set up and executed was smooth and effective. But they weren't quite sure *how* it had been done. The coach stood and looking at the boss said, "What just happened?"

"You gave me feedback on what I did, but it was more than just feedback. It was more powerful in some way."

"And that's exactly what it is, *more powerful.* And because it's more powerful, it is more effective. I could have said 'atta boy,' or 'atta girl,' or 'way to go,' or 'nice going,' or 'keep it up,' or 'looking good.' And all of those comments are perhaps good, and many people feel better after hearing them. But they lack the power we oftentimes need to get the reaction we want. I call 'atta boys' or 'atta girls' *insignificant feedback,* because they lack the power of real supportive feedback."

The coach walked to the side of the room where a large poster board was tacked to the wall. She removed the front to expose a formula.

Pointing to each step in succession, the coach said, "First, I described specifically what you did, in other words, your behavior. Next, I explained the positive consequences of that behavior. Then I told you how I feel about what you did. And finally, I explained why I feel the way I do. Each of the four steps is designed to focus the supportive feedback in a way to maximize its effect. An 'atta boy' is less effective than this formula because it is so nonspecific and unfocused. The recipient of an 'atta boy' may not be able to connect your feedback with his or her behavior. The reason this formula works so well is that it supports the specific behavior that you want repeated, and it does so in a very powerful way."

The coach then slid her chair to a position directly in front of the manager whose assistant had only recently begun centering

Figure 7-3. Four steps of supportive feedback.

Steps of Supportive Feedback:
1. Describe the specific behavior.
2. Describe the consequences of the behavior.
3. Describe how you feel about the behavior.
4. Describe why you feel that way.

headers on computer reports. Giving the manager an encouraging smile, the coach said, "As my administrative assistant, I know that you struggled with the way that I like computer reports formatted. But these latest reports are really nice! When I refer to them to get information, like in a meeting, this formatting is much easier for me. And I want you to know how much I appreciate what you've done, because I think it will make both of our jobs easier."

Next the coach moved her chair in front of the manager who had been working with a vendor and continued her demonstrations of supportive feedback. "These past few weeks I've noticed that you have gone out of your way to help me. I particularly appreciate the way that you have included more detail on your invoices so that I can match the charges and get them approved for payment. It saves me time and has made an otherwise unpleasant task quite enjoyable."

The coach walked back to the front of the room and continued, "Sometimes you can't see the actual behavior, such as the son who cleans his bedroom while you are on a business trip. But if you pay attention to a person's performance, you can see the *result* of the behavior. In the three cases I just demonstrated, I actually reinforced the *behaviors* and the *results*, because in each case I would like both repeated."

The coach added, "The consequences of a person's behavior can often be described by how the behavior impacts others in the organization or the family. A son is more likely to keep his bedroom clean if he clearly understands that his behaviors have a significant impact on other family members. The administrative assistant is more likely to center headers on a computer report if that person understands how much I like them centered. Vendors are more likely to deliver on time and cause fewer problems when they understand how their behaviors impact our organization."

The coach looked at the manager who earlier said that giving feedback wasn't rocket science and said, "So there's a lot we can learn about giving supportive feedback to others. It may not be rocket science, but it does take a little practice for us to be able to deliver it in a powerful way."

Looking down, and then back to the group, the coach added a final thought. "But sometimes, with some people, supportive feedback doesn't work. In spite of your best efforts, whether you use the power formula or not, some people won't react positively to supportive feedback. What do you do then? Is there a formula for those situations? Well, we'll answer these questions in our next session. See you then."

Corrective Feedback—The Tough One

The group of managers assembled in the meeting room a couple of weeks later for another class with the coach. A message had been written on the whiteboard before anyone arrived. It said: "We have an important task ahead of us today."

Below the words a poster board was stuck to the whiteboard and seemed to cover something.

The boss made a few introductory comments and then turned the time over to the coach. But before he was able to take his seat, she asked, "How are your sons' bedrooms?"

"Not bad," he said. "I wouldn't say that they're where my wife and I would like them, but the younger boy's room is quite a bit better, and the older boy's room is showing signs of improvement."

Figure 8-1. Important task.

"We have an important task ahead of us today."

The coach nodded and commented, "In an e-mail a few days ago you told me about your youngest son wanting some glass cleaner."

"Oh yeah, each day I've kept up the supportive feedback to my younger son by filling his bucket. He cleaned a little, and I reinforced a little. And with each improvement I could see a change in his attitude about other things. Things like his chores around the house, how he treats his mother, homework, and those sorts of things. Then one night he asked his mother what she used to clean windows. She asked him what he wanted glass cleaner for, and he said that he wanted to clean the windows in his room."

"The windows?"

"Yeah, his bedroom windows! You know that I've been converted to this way of thinking for some time now, but when I heard about the glass cleaner, I became a committed convert."

"A committed convert. I'll have to add that to my script."

"Before we move on, I've got to ask something. You said that after you reinforced the fourteen-year-old's spontaneous improvement his cleaning improved even more. And you repeated that process several times. Is that correct?"

"That's what happened."

"I heard you say that after the cycle was repeated a couple of times you noticed an improvement in other areas of his life. You mentioned doing chores, treating his mother better, and homework. Is that correct?"

"It is. His behavior changed in more ways than just cleaning his bedroom."

"So what can happen when an employee receives supportive feedback for even spontaneous improvement?"

"I think we could experience improvement in areas unrelated to the specific feedback. Sounds interesting." This possibility obviously intrigued the boss.

The coach turned from the boss and asked the managers,

"Did you all get the significance of what we just heard? All from a garbage sack and some slightly used pizza boxes!"

Two Directions

The coach moved to a table in the center of the room and continued. "In the business world there are two directions you can take when giving supportive feedback. You can reinforce who the person is inside, or you can reinforce a behavior the person exhibits that you would like repeated. Although both of these reinforcements are good and appropriate, knowing when to use each type, and how much of it to do, can be confusing."

The coach looked from one manager to another and asked, "How can you know if people need to be supported for who they *are*, or supported for what they have *done?*"

When nobody seemed ready to answer the question, the coach answered it herself. "In some ways, giving feedback is a challenge, because being able to read other people and how they react to feedback increases your ability to deliver it. And, as I hope we all know, being able to accurately read other people isn't an innate skill that most of us have. It's something we have to develop.

"So how can a manager, or parent for that matter, know whether it's best to reinforce a behavior or reinforce the person?"

A tall, heavyset manager propped up his hand on the table and said, "I thought about that a lot after our last session. It seems impossible to tell at first, but I think a good communicator probably does both. I'm not sure if it's in equal amounts or not, but I'm sure a good manager would have to do both."

"I agree. It can take some time and practice in reading people to be able to discern how much reinforcement of a behavior is needed as compared to reinforcing the person's desirable character traits. Perhaps the reason it can be confusing is that both of these reinforcements are necessary. The challenge is deciding when to use each type."

The coach paused for a minute and finished her thought, "Actually, the two techniques are related. So whether you reinforce the person, or the behavior, you haven't wasted your time. Good things frequently happen as a result of either type of supportive feedback. Beyond trying to mix the two types of feedback with a person, I usually reinforce the behavior if I'm able to give the feedback immediately after the behavior. Otherwise, I use a mixture of the two methods."

The Pressure for Profit

The coach held up some papers that had been stapled together for the class to see. She said, "This is a profit and loss statement from one of my clients. The business world revolves around P&L statements just like this one. I'm sure this company has one and it is probably a standard yardstick for most people."

After placing the P&L on the table, she continued, "Quite frankly, because of the pressure to produce profit in the business world, too many managers have forgotten the importance of helping employees reduce or eliminate ineffective behaviors. One of the most effective ways I know of eliminating ineffective behaviors from employees is to fill their feedback buckets. When your supportive feedback fills someone's bucket and makes the person feel good inside, there is a much better chance that that person will act effectively and cause fewer problems in the future. In other words, a little investment of your time today will likely bring fewer problems tomorrow. And fewer problems mean an improvement in the bottom line on the P&L. This means that delivering effective feedback is directly related to business profit."

This Isn't Easy

After the group returned from a break, with a small grin on her face the coach announced, "Now I think it's time to see how much you've learned in our classes. What can appear as simple theory in giving feedback can actually be fairly difficult to put into practice. So, I'm going to ask a couple of volunteers to show us what they think corrective feedback looks like."

The coach moved two chairs into a V formation at the front of the room and said, "I need two volunteers." She paused a few seconds while she looked over the group. "How about the two of you coming down to demonstrate your skills?" She had pointed toward the tall, heavyset man and a woman wearing a brown pantsuit sitting next to him.

As they took their seats, the coach gave them their assignment. "Sir, you are an employee who has both behavior and performance issues. But that isn't a problem because you don't think it's a big deal. This is your manager, who has tried supportive feedback for the past few weeks, but for whatever reason you have ignored her thus far. She is now going to role-play as your manager in an attempt to correct your behavior. As her employee, you just play along the way an employee would, and let's see what happens."

The woman didn't miss a beat and said almost instantly, "Thanks for coming. We need to discuss some things that have been going on around the office. There was an incident yesterday and another one this morning where you became angry with other employees. I'm told that you snapped at people because you were frustrated about something. I don't really think it's productive for us to get into a debate about who said what, and who did what."

The role-playing manager paused for a couple of seconds to collect her thoughts, then continued, "I'm sure you know how important it is that we get along with each other around here. And I'm sure you want to be part of a team environment where people experience mutual respect, which will enable our company to grow strong in the marketplace. Don't you agree?"

The tall manager, playing the role of the employee, shrugged and said, "Well, I guess so." It looked as though he was having fun playing the part of a low-performing employee.

Looking for help, the manager glanced at the poster boards on the walls and then continued, "I need you to correct your behavior so that we can achieve the results that we need so that we can meet our corporate goals."

The manager paused, wondering if the coach had set her up in an unwinnable situation. While she pondered where to go next, her employee asked, "So what are you going to do if I do the same thing again?"

There were several smiles in the room while the manager felt a sinking feeling in her heart. Having absolutely no idea what to say, she volunteered, "Well, if we continue to see these problems in the future, I guess you will be conducting blue-light specials at your local Kmart store."

After the laughter died down, the coach interrupted the role-play to thank the two "volunteers," and asked them to return to their original chairs. She was smiling, too. The blue-light comment was obviously humorous to her as well. Collecting herself, she asked, "My, we seem to have covered all of our bases there."

"Tell me," the coach said, "other than her affinity for blue lights, what do you think about the effectiveness of our manager's attempt to apply corrective feedback?"

The tall manager who played the role of the employee spoke first. "I had the feeling she was telling me what I had to do as a condition of employment."

"It appeared to you as though you were being *told* what had to change," the coach summarized.

Another manager said, "I got the impression that she was trying to *convince* the employee to change his behavior."

"You saw it as *persuasion* then."

"Yeah, if you don't mind my poetry: She *told* him and then she *sold* him."

"I agree, she did both of those. And there was something else she did that involved the blue-light special. What was that?"

A manager sitting on the back side of the U table formation

said, "It doesn't rhyme, but she *told* him, *sold* him, and then *threatened* him."

"That's what I was looking for. Now to our two volunteers, please don't be offended, because both of you did exactly what I was hoping you would do. We appreciate and applaud your Academy Award performances."

Common Methods of Changing Behavior

There was a little applause while the coach walked to a wall where she removed another poster board. There was a list written on the whiteboard.

The coach pulled up a chair and sat down. It looked as though she was about to have a chat with a friend. "Left to our own devices, most of us try to correct the behavior of others by *telling* or *selling*. And if those fail, we resort to *threatening*. It's as common as a new CEO wanting his or her picture on the front page of the company newsletter."

She nodded her head and continued. "Now perhaps a new CEO should be pictured on the front page of the newsletter, but the problem is that telling, selling, and threatening are only marginally effective. And if they work at all, it's only until you turn your back. Then the person often goes right back to the same old behavior. If you doubt that, consider *your* reaction to being told what to do. Isn't your first reaction to being told *what, when,* or *how* one of recoiling or standing firm against the request? And

Figure 8-2. Traditional methods to change behavior.

Traditional Methods Used to Change Behavior:
- Telling
- Selling
- Threatening

then, how do you feel about being *sold* on something? I know it makes me feel inferior or unqualified in some manner. My natural defensive instincts kick in when someone tries to sell me something."

The coach held up her outstretched hands and asked, "And then what do you think about being threatened? 'There will be dire consequences if you don't immediately change your behavior.' Now, if what I've done is serious enough, I might accept a line being drawn in the sand. But what if I don't believe my behavior deserves a threat? How effective will a threat be then?"

Pausing a few seconds for her words to sink in, the coach asked, "Telling, selling, and threatening: what do you think?"

A number of managers spoke at once. Their interest was high and most had opinions they wished to share. One manager won out and spoke first. "I feel like I have egg on my face because that's exactly what I do. If I like the person a lot, I try to sell them on a change. If I like them a little, I tell them what has to change. And if I don't care much for them, I'm sure I resort to threats."

"So what should we do?" another manager asked.

The woman who played the role of the manager said, "Some employees will only respond to what you call a line drawn in the sand."

Another manager added, "There are employees who are only here for a paycheck. They couldn't care less about the company. And sometimes the only way you can get their attention is to threaten them."

"Okay, okay, I give up!" The coach held up her hands in submission and walked to the center of the room and continued her thought. "Remember, changing behavior is a process. Sometimes it can be a slow process. And sometimes it won't work, despite our best efforts. But remember, our obligation as managers and leaders is to use the best techniques we can."

The coach paused to collect her thoughts and continued, "Over many years of dealing with people—some cooperative and some less than cooperative—I have developed a series of steps that can be used in a progression from mild intervention to serious intervention. You already should have guessed that the first step in this progression is to try supportive feedback. But now what do you do if that doesn't work?"

Steps of Corrective Feedback

The coach walked to the whiteboard and removed a poster board. Now revealed on the whiteboard were the steps of corrective feedback.

She explained, "Now that we've discussed supportive feedback, we're going to look at the other steps in the process. Remember, changing behavior is almost always a process, especially in difficult situations."

The coach took a couple of steps toward the group and continued. "At the first indication that behaviors need to be changed, it's usually a good strategy to try supportive feedback first. I've been surprised in many situations where supportive feedback by itself corrected the problem. I know it defies reason, but in select situations, it works. In this class we've seen an account rep named Jerry change his behavior with supportive feedback, and we've heard about a fourteen-year-old son who has been cleaning his bedroom lately, including the windows, also because of supportive feedback."

Figure 8-3. Five steps to correct behavior.

Steps of Corrective Feedback:
1. Try supportive feedback first.
2. Use carefully guided questions.
3. State that improvement is needed.
4. Use appropriate discipline.
5. Draw a line in the sand.

Pointing to the first item on the chart indicating supportive feedback, she continued, "So if the situation permits, begin the corrective process with your best supportive feedback. And if that doesn't work in a reasonable amount of time, move on to the next step. But remember, I can't tell you how many times in my career I've found that supportive feedback changed the desired behavior before I needed to try something else."

Moving her hand to the next line on the board, she continued, "In a few minutes I'll demonstrate for you a technique of asking carefully guided questions that has great power to change behavior. But let me briefly describe the other steps on this list before I do that. Sometimes the power of good questions won't work with some people. So there is a technique of stating in an assertive way what you need changed."

The coach changed her tone of voice a little and continued, "There is a part of corrective feedback that both managers and parents call discipline. Technically, discipline is corrective feedback, because the discipline is administered in an attempt to change behavior. We all know from experience that on occasion, in selected situations, it is necessary and appropriate to apply discipline. To do otherwise can create a climate of permissiveness that has overwhelming negative consequences. And having to deal with the negative consequences of a permissive climate is a whole different problem."

The coach underlined the final line on the board with her hand and added, "The final step on this list is to draw a line in the sand. This isn't a class in how to apply discipline, but let me just say that the best way I've found to use this last step is to say to the employee that I've now been backed into a corner and if he or she doesn't correct the problem immediately I will be left with only one choice. And I let the employee ponder what that one possibility might be. An employee's punitive assumptions can be far greater than my actual intentions."

"Let me summarize what I've just said." The coach paused.

"Effective communicators will always try supportive feedback first—just like your boss did with his assignment in his sons' bedrooms. If that doesn't work, then one of the steps of corrective feedback is appropriate. And if corrective feedback doesn't work, then discipline is warranted."

The coach noticed that the boss seemed to have a puzzled look on his face. She turned toward him and said, "I can see by the expression on your face that you've got a question almost ready to be asked."

"Well, actually, I do. If supportive feedback, corrective feedback, and discipline are all so closely related, shouldn't all three of them be part of our company's progressive discipline policy?"

"What do you think?"

"I think we need to think about that," the boss said.

"I agree," the coach replied, "but few executives I've encountered have ever considered that."

Behavior, Performance, and Results

Turning back to the managers, the coach walked to another wall where a poster board was also stuck to another whiteboard. She removed the poster board, which revealed what looked like a formula. "It's important to understand how feedback should be applied for most people so that you can know when to use supportive feedback or corrective feedback. Years ago this chart helped me understand the difference."

The coach turned to face the group and said, "The reason why we need to support or correct behaviors is that behaviors drive performance, and performance drives results. The process works like this."

She pointed toward the top two lines and continued. "Positive behaviors tend to drive positive performance, which tends to drive positive results, which *deserves* supportive feedback, or the positive behavior may not be repeated."

Figure 8-4. Appropriate reaction to positive and negative behaviors.

Positive Behavior	→	Positive Performance	→	Positive Results	→	Supportive Feedback
Negative Behavior	→	Negative Performance	→	Negative Results	→	Corrective Feedback

Moving on to the bottom two lines she added, "Negative behaviors tend to drive negative performance, which tends to drive negative results, which *deserves* corrective feedback."

Gesturing to the formula on the wall, the coach concluded, "If supportive feedback doesn't work, then move on to corrective feedback. If corrective feedback doesn't work, then move on to drawing a line in the sand with an appropriate level of discipline. Over time, you will become more adept in knowing when to give each type of feedback. For the time being, do your best."

The Dinner Date

During a break Scott approached the coach, but before he could say anything, she said, "These classes are murder on my feet, so while you stand for a rest, I need to sit for a rest."

Scott smiled and said, "A lot of what we discussed on the phone and in e-mails makes more sense after that discussion."

"Your supportive feedback with Jerry was the right answer, but there was a small possibility that it might not have worked. That can happen in almost any situation due to the differences in people." The coach took a second look at Scott, as he stood before her, and asked, "How did your special assignment at home turn out?"

"I can tell you're referring to the apology. I used what I

learned with Jerry on my wife. We went on a date to dinner because food always works when I have something important to say.
It set the right mood and I apologized to her for what I had been
doing and promised her that I would do much better in the future."

"How did she respond?"

"I think the best way to describe her response would be tenta-
tive, but we clearly made more progress that night, and since, than
we have in several years. I like those three steps: Eliminate the
critical, increase the supportive, and apologize when appropriate.
They may have saved my marriage and my relationship with my
kids. Not to mention what happened with Jerry. Thanks!"

"You're welcome. It's nice to hear such a good report."

With a trace of a smile on his face, Scott said, "You told me a
few weeks ago not to give up on the feedback at home, so I
haven't. I've learned that it's important not to give up."

The coach stood up and said, "I like what I'm hearing."

Before he walked to the refreshments, Scott looked back at
the coach and said, "Thanks, *Dr. Feedback*, for giving me feedback." With a raised eyebrow, the coach smiled.

Corrective Feedback with Questions

After the break, the coach continued, "Thanks to the role-playing
we witnessed, you know that telling, selling, and threatening are
ineffective methods of changing behavior. In a few minutes we'll
talk about making assertive statements, but now let's look at my
favorite method—asking guided questions."

The coach pushed an extra chair to a position across the table
from where the boss was seated. She sat down, pointed toward the
boss, and said, "I'd like you to meet my seventeen-year-old son.
Let's call him Junior, because he looks so much like his name-
sake." Pointing toward herself, she continued, "And I'd like you

to meet Junior's dad; that would be me." There were several chuckles in the room at the inference.

The coach looked at the boss and explained, "I'd like you to role-play a situation with me. You play the part of your son, and I'll be you. I've given my best shot at positive feedback, but it hasn't worked, so now I'm going to use the technique of guided questions as corrective feedback in order to change your behavior. The situation is my son's future. He seems to lack direction in his life and spends too much time doing what to me are unproductive activities. I'm concerned that he doesn't have a plan for his future."

The coach turned around to face most of the managers and added, "Your responsibility while we do this role-play demonstration is to diagnose *how* it's done. So watch carefully to see how guided questions can change behavior."

Turning back to Junior, she began, "Thanks for coming with me to get some pizza. There is something important that I'd like to discuss with you. I'm concerned about what appears to be a lack of direction in your life. You're seventeen now and graduation from high school is only a few months away. What would you like to be doing a year from now?"

"I dunno," Junior (the boss) said, as if he had heard that phrase a million times. Several of the managers laughed, because they had obviously heard the same response from their own kids.

Seemingly unfazed by the comment, she continued, "I think you do know. I know you like to be with your friends, and you like to work with computers and play computer games. You know what you like, and what you don't like. So you've probably given a little thought to next year. I respect you, so I'll respect your answer. What would you like to be doing in a year?"

"I guess going to school."

"Going to school is a really good answer. What, then, would you like to be doing in five years?"

"Five years after I start school, I guess I would be graduated."

"That's where you'll *be* in five years. Tell me what you would like to be *doing* in five years."

The boss looked toward the other managers in the room and began, "I assume I'm not allowed to say, 'I dunno.'"

"That's right," the coach quickly agreed.

The boss moved back to his role as Junior. "Some of my friends know exactly what they want to do, but I'm not sure. It might be something with computers."

"So some of your friends already have a direction in mind. How do you feel about your friends knowing what they want to do, and you being undecided?"

"It bothers me."

"It sounds like you're bothered by not knowing, but if you chose today, it might be something in the computer field."

"That's right."

"Some people can get confused about a solution to a problem, because they can't see all the minute details to the solution. It's possible that the problem you're having deciding is in part based on how wide and complex the computer field has become. How close am I?"

"Well, it is large, and I'm not sure if I want to work in systems, networks, programming, or whatever. I just don't know."

"That is exactly my point. I would be confused, too. Most people would." The coach, taking this role very seriously, moved forward on her chair, and continued, "The question for now is, is it absolutely necessary for a first-year computer student to decide his specialty before he begins any classes? What do you think?"

"I hadn't thought about that. Maybe it's not."

"I'm sure it's not. So if you would like to be graduated with some type of a degree in computers in five years, and you would like to be working toward that goal one year from today by going to school, what do you need to do this week, or this month in order to help you achieve your goals?"

"Get ready for graduation and send in my application to the community college."

"That's exactly right. What could I do to help?"

A Ton of Questions

The coach stood up and broke her concentration on the role-play. "Wow!" she said. "We have another actor in our group."

The boss added, "That wasn't acting. That was the real thing. I'm thinking about going back to school and making a career change!"

"I think somebody had better warn the school if he's coming," a manager shouted out, laughing.

The coach liked the way this group could interact with each other in a fun and nonthreatening manner. The open communication of good-natured teasing and sharing their feelings these managers demonstrated was a strong indication of team cohesiveness. She said, "Back to Junior and his dad. What technique did I use as I attempted to correct his behavior?"

"You asked a ton of questions," Scott said.

"And what do questions do to a discussion like that?"

"You just asked another one," a manager added.

"That I did, but what purpose do they serve when you are trying to change behavior?"

"There's another one!" someone added.

Scott took the lead and said, "It looked like your questions let you almost direct the discussion without appearing to be overly controlling. The questions also got the other person talking."

Problem and Solution Ownership

The coach looked over the group of managers and asked, "When I ask an employee to describe a situation that has become a problem, who is most likely to have psychological *ownership* of that problem: me or the employee?"

"The employee," a manager responded.

"Then, when I ask a series of guided questions that cause the employee to volunteer a solution to his or her problem, who *owns* the solution?"

"The employee," the same manager said.

"And if I resort to *telling* or *selling* the employee on the problem and solution, who has psychological ownership?"

"You do," the same manager said.

"In our role-play a minute ago, who *controlled* the discussion?" the coach asked.

"You did. Your questions provided the direction."

"Always remember that the person asking questions guides the direction of the discussion—that's why I refer to this technique as asking guided questions. What purpose did the one-year and five-year questions serve?"

It was Scott who answered this time. "They forced Junior to move his attention from the problems of today and think about where he wants to be tomorrow."

"They clearly did that, but what does all of this have to do with keeping his bedroom clean?"

No one spoke. The question caught everyone by surprise. The only sound in the room was the constant hum from the fluorescent light fixtures in the ceiling. When nobody spoke up, the coach said, "Living in serious clutter or even filth is often related to the perception a person has of him or herself. So if Junior is unsure about his future, as he seems to be, why should he worry about the physical conditions of where he sleeps each night? I'll bet an ice cream cone that when Junior finds his direction in college and improves his self-perception, he will find his direction in his bedroom, too. That will be especially true if he receives consistent supportive feedback from his parents. So keep the glass cleaner handy!"

Assertive Statements to Correct Behavior

The coach reached under one of the side tables and brought out another poster board. She hung it on the front wall and said, "I ran out of walls for these posters so I saved this one for last."

The coach continued, "There are situations where neither supportive feedback nor asking questions will get the desired behavior change. Some people are stubborn. Some situations are difficult or even explosive. Sometimes things don't go as planned. Whatever the reason, you need a direct technique that can work in those situations. I've seen this final technique work in situations where the others failed. Notice that it is very similar to the supportive feedback strategy that we learned earlier."

The coach walked to a position in front of the boss and pushed aside the chair where she had been seated a few minutes earlier. She looked down at the boss and said, "Junior, for several years you have neglected your bedroom. There are dirty clothes and discarded food wrappers on the floor. Your room hasn't been cleaned for a long time. You have lived with trash and clutter for so long that I fear it has become a way of life. Quite frankly, I feel embarrassed to have anyone see your room, because it lowers the standard of our entire family. I need you to take better care of your room. What can I do to help?"

After her demonstration of the technique, the coach turned

Figure 8-5. Using assertive statements to correct behavior.

Assertive Statements Used as Corrective Feedback:
1. Describe the specific behavior.
2. Describe the consequences of the behavior.
3. Describe how you feel about the behavior.
4. Describe why you feel that way.
5. Describe what you need changed.

to the other class members and asked, "What do you think? Would that work?"

The boss said, "I like the asking questions technique. I think Junior, as you call him, would respond better to being asked, rather than being told."

"That's good insight. Who else has a thought?"

Another manager said, "Junior might respond better to being asked with guided questions, but it looks like what you just did was a last resort, after everything else failed. I've had employees over the years who needed to be told. I wish I had known how to tell them assertively, as you call it. Corrective feedback would probably have worked better than my threats."

"That's the point," the coach said. "Understanding how to communicate corrective feedback gives you options. And those options enable you to become a more effective person—both at work and at home."

The meeting broke up shortly after that, and on his way out Scott heard the coach say, "I'll be looking forward to hearing about your progress on those assignments."

Scott just nodded, because he knew what she meant.

CHAPTER 9

The Challenge Is Making It Happen

Scott wondered if something was wrong. His boss practiced something he called "leading by walking around." He tried to communicate with his staff as much as he could by visiting them in their offices at their location, rather than summoning them to his office. Being summoned to an executive's office could have, he said, a negative impact on open communications. That's why you would see the boss making personal visits to offices in the building so that he could communicate on the employee's turf, rather than his own. Scott liked the idea and had been emulating his boss in that way for some time. So when he received a message that he was needed ASAP in his boss's office, he was clearly concerned. The elevators were too slow, so he decided to use a stairway. As he raced up the back stairs he dialed his wife's cell phone. He was almost in a state of panic until she finally answered on the fifth ring. But she said everything with her and the children was fine. So whatever the problem was, it wasn't something at home. What else could be wrong? He didn't have a clue what was going on.

As he burst through the door to the executive offices on the fifth floor of his company's office building, he was immediately reminded of how much he liked the décor of that floor. It wasn't that his office on the third floor was in poor taste or badly designed. It was just that the furnishings and color scheme of the fifth floor were so striking. As he began walking toward the corner office on the far side of the stairway, he was even struck with the quiet of this floor. The view out the large windows was incredible. A dense forest lined the building on the back side and gave it a secluded setting in the business park.

When he approached the corner office, an executive assistant said, "Go right in, Scott. They're waiting for you." Scott thought, *They are waiting for me. Who is waiting for me?*

As he entered he could see his boss and the coach sitting at a round side table. Papers were spread out and they had obviously been engaged in a discussion.

"Come in, Scott. We need your help," his boss said. "Have a seat."

The coach followed with, "It's good to see you. Thanks for the e-mail updates. Putting a month between the last two sessions has cut into my involvement, so I enjoy reading your e-mails." The coach paused a couple of seconds and asked, "How are you doing with your daughter?"

Scott sat down in an empty chair at the small table and glanced at his boss because he didn't know how much his boss knew about the situation. The coach, sensing that Scott might be uncomfortable discussing a personal matter in that setting, quickly added, "Scott and I have had a few conversations regarding his relationship with his ten-year-old daughter."

"That's great," his boss said. "So how are you and your daughter doing?"

Scott briefly explained how she hadn't initially reacted to his attempts at improved feedback. Then he added, "Things began to change for the better when I balanced the types of feedback I gave to her." Scott looked at the coach and continued, "The three things you challenged me to do—they made the difference."

The coach took a few seconds while she looked at Scott. It was as if she were considering something. "How are you two doing now?" she persisted.

"We talk. We're beginning to do things. I listen. She's including me a little in her life. And most important I've seen her laugh. It's not where I would like it to be yet, but like you said, it'll take some time to repair the damage I did for the first ten years. I really appreciate your help."

"That's wonderful, Scott," his boss said. "As I said several months ago at the beginning of this process, when we help one of our people with their problems at home, we also help them with their productivity at work. So I'm really pleased that you and your daughter are doing better."

Then changing the subject he added, "Scott, the final meeting for this first group of managers and our coach is next week. I want all of our managers and supervisors to go through the class on feedback, and I'd like you to head up that project by being the facilitator for the next group."

So this was why he had been summoned to the corner office on the fifth floor. His imagination and insecurity had caused him to assume the worst, but it was good news, not bad. But he didn't understand what his boss meant. So with a puzzled look on his face Scott asked, "What do you mean, facilitator?"

"Facilitator is the role I've played in our current session. It just means that you introduce our coach and make sure the people get the most out of the process. You might get a few assignments yourself, just like I did."

"I'd love to do that. I appreciate your confidence that I could be the facilitator."

Smiling and nodding her head, the coach said, "Scott, you'll do great. It's been exciting to watch how well you've taken to the power of positive feedback."

Nodding his agreement, the boss added, "I concur. There is no question that you should be the facilitator for the next class. Here's a list of people we've been working on. Look it over, compare calendars, and let me know who should be there and when you want to hold the first session."

As Scott was leaving the corner office, his boss grinned and asked, "By the way, in the first session are you going to have someone go to the front desk for an envelope?"

Scott smiled at the coach and replied, "Oh yeah, the infamous envelope. Well, it worked for me."

Time to Support

On his way down the stairs to the third floor, Scott's words to the coach kept ringing in his ears: *"It worked for me."* Yes, it had worked for him. So many things in his life were working better for him. And it all seemed to revolve around using supportive and corrective feedback effectively, minimizing insignificant feedback, and eliminating abusive feedback.

Then, as he entered the landing for the fourth floor, a thought crossed his mind. "Speaking of envelopes, there is something I need to do. And it'll only take a minute," he said aloud to himself.

Earlier that week a new clerk whom he hadn't seen before brought an envelope to his office that had been misdirected to the fourth floor. That misdirection by someone in the mailroom, combined with what appeared to be a misprint by the sender on the addressee line, had delayed some critical information that Scott really needed. He had called the mailroom supervisor three times looking for the envelope, but it couldn't be found.

Then the new clerk from the fourth floor showed up at his office with a question. "Pardon me, sir. I hate to bother you, but I've been asking around and I think this might be the missing envelope you were asking about. It was sent to an office on the fourth floor by mistake, but I'm pretty sure it fits the description of what you are looking for."

It was indeed the missing envelope, and thanks to an alert new employee, Scott was able to salvage a potentially expensive situation. He had told the clerk how much he appreciated getting the envelope, but that's all he had done. Now it was time to make feedback work in someone else's life, too.

After cornering the new clerk and the clerk's supervisor on the fourth floor, Scott said, "I just wanted you to know how valuable your alertness has been to me and our company. Even being a new employee, you were alert enough to hear about a missing envelope and kept your eyes open for it. Then, finding it, you sought me out to deliver it in person. Because of your attention to detail, a potentially expensive problem was prevented. It really makes me feel great to know that we are hiring people who have that much persistence, because it makes the entire organization that much stronger. Thank you so much."

After Scott had delivered his supportive statement, the clerk expressed appreciation for Scott's thoughtfulness. But the real payback came a few hours later when the new clerk's supervisor called Scott and said, "My new employee was flabbergasted hearing what you said. He told me that this is a neat place to work because the higher-ups take the time to tell you when you do a good job. He really didn't expect to hear anything more about the envelope. Apparently he felt unappreciated at his last job, and that was why he left."

Manager in the Hallway

A couple of days later Scott heard someone call out his name as he walked down a hallway. Turning around, he saw his friend—the manager who could only see his son on alternate weekends. Scott had some pressing issues, but he knew he needed to spend a minute with this colleague.

After shaking hands and exchanging a few pleasantries, Scott asked, "How are you doing with your son?"

"About the same, except that I keep trying to use some of the techniques we've learned on positive feedback. I think I'm making progress, but it's hard to tell. By the way, thanks for your encouragement the other day."

"I'm glad I could help. I'm sorry you only see him every other weekend. I can tell how important he is to you."

His feelings close to the surface, the manager glanced down at the floor for a couple of seconds and then up at Scott and nodded.

Then the manager said, "I've learned a lot in our classes. I'm sorry there's only one class left. I feel like I could use more help."

"The company is going to offer another series of sessions on feedback with our coach. I've been asked to head up the next group of our managers. Even though you've already been through the sessions, you're welcome to come again. We'd love to have you there."

"That might work. I'll have to look at my schedule. Say, I've been going to a counselor for the last month trying to resolve some of the issues about the divorce, and she said something that reminded me of something you said. She told me that I lack *positive self-talk,* where I tell myself that I'm a good person and that the direction I'm going now is okay. And after what we've learned about feedback, it sounds to me that positive self-talk is nothing more than giving yourself positive feedback. Isn't that right?"

Scott didn't know for sure, but it made sense to him. So he replied, "I think you're right. If other people can give you feedback, I'm sure you can give it to yourself, too."

"At the end of my first session with the counselor she said that I had so much guilt for what had happened that I was condemning myself with self-doubt. She said that my self-talk was negative and that I needed to turn it around to positive. She explained that, 'positive thoughts lead to positive behaviors, and negative thoughts lead to negative behaviors.' And that's basically the same message we've learned in our classes."

The coach hadn't discussed self-talk in the feedback classes, but Scott could see the value in what his friend had just said. It must be true. A few of his own thoughts came back to him, thoughts of several months ago when his life was much different than the way it was today. He could recall thinking to himself that each and every aspect of his life wasn't working. He could recall making mental lists of things that didn't work, rather than lists of things that did work. In the past few months many things in his life had changed—for the better.

"You're right," he said to his friend. "You can give yourself feedback, and whether you choose positive or abusive feedback can influence how you'll behave afterward. That's because feedback is so directly connected to behavior."

"I appreciate the advice," his friend said, "but now you sound like the coach teaching our classes! Say, I have a question. I've been using the supportive feedback on my son when he visits for the weekend. But something is wrong, because we still don't connect. Our interests are so different that when he's at my house, it's like we're strangers. The feedback helps—but something is missing."

Scott could relate to what he had just heard. It sounded like the same problem he had had with his daughter. "With my daughter I learned that I had to become interested in what she wanted to do. I couldn't expect her to be interested in what I wanted to do or talk about. The same thing is true for my son. If he wants to play catch in the backyard, that's what I've got to do in order to invest time in our relationship. So whatever he wants to talk about, that's what I have to make as my priority. If you want to improve your relationship with your son, you'll have to do things that he's interested in. In fact, the same thing is true here at work with our employees."

"But all my son wants to do is play video games. I bought a new system for him so he will have a good one when he visits me."

Scott had been there before, so he asked, "Does the new video game have one paddle control or two?"

"It's got two, but I don't like kids' games. I don't even like computer games."

"Whether you like kids' games or not isn't the point. The best time to give kids feedback is while relating to them on their level, not yours. So if you want your feedback to have a powerful impact on your son, you'll have to pick up a controller and play the games with him. That will give you an opportunity to support what you like, and correct what needs to be improved. You'll also find that after you invest time doing what he wants he'll be more willing to invest time doing what you want."

"You think?"

"I know! I've been there with my kids, my wife, and my employees! Trust me."

Time to Correct

Scott realized that he needed to keep a promise. Several months ago he had promised Jerry that he would support when it was appropriate, and correct when it was appropriate. And since he had made that promise he had held true to his word. Now there was a situation with Jerry where it would be appropriate to use corrective feedback. It was time.

Jerry's workstation didn't afford much privacy. There white noise from the ceiling, and padded dividers separated him from the next person, but sometimes conversations could be overheard. So Scott met Jerry in a small conference room so that he could adhere to the adage, "praise in public and correct in private."

"Jerry, we need to talk about your Weekly Client Contact Re-

ports. The last two reports have been late by several days, and it
appears to be the same problem we experienced two months ago.
Help me understand what's going on."

"I thought you'd be asking about that. The last time I put
them off too long, but these last two weeks I've been swamped
with some back orders and I just didn't get them in. I'm sorry."

"Do you know that when your report is late I have to guess
what contacts you've made and add it to my report? I really feel
uncomfortable having to guess about those numbers because it
makes the whole process for our division flawed."

Scott paused a minute to make sure that he was handling this
situation properly. Continuing, he asked, "Tell me, what could we
work out so that they would be on time in the future?"

"To be honest, the real problem is that sometimes when I get
back from a trip I'm really bushed and I don't bring my laptop
into my home office. I leave it in my car. Then I get busy with
other things and the report doesn't get done until I bring the
laptop in here. It's really my fault."

"So what's the solution?" Scott asked.

"I've just got to be more conscientious in getting the reports
e-mailed to you on time. That's all."

"I agree. Help me understand how we can do that."

"There's nothing you can do. It's my job. I've just got to make
it a higher priority and get it done."

"That sounds good, Jerry. You are clear, aren't you, that when
I don't have the real numbers, I have to plug in my own guesses?"

"Actually, I didn't know that, but I do now. It's just something that I've got to do. And I will. I'll make it happen!"

"Thanks, Jerry. I appreciate you and what you do for our
division. Be sure to let me know if I can do anything for you."

"Thanks, Scott. I appreciate you, too."

After Jerry left the conference room, Scott reflected on how
he had handled the correction. Pretty well overall, he thought.

Much better than he would have handled it six months ago. Yep, things were going better. Much better.

Graduation

There were more refreshments than there had been at the previous sessions, and the table was decorated with multicolored helium-filled balloons. As a show of support, the president of the company was there. It was going to be a happy occasion. The tall, heavyset manager hardly ever wore a suit jacket to work, unless it was something special. He was wearing a jacket today, even though it looked a couple of sizes too small.

The boss made a few comments, followed by the president. They both believed in the process and encouraged the participants not to forget what they had learned. In his comments the boss said, "Our company has invested in your ability to deal more effectively with other people. Throughout the process of classes and homework, we've been unable to separate being effective at home from being effective at work. That's because the skills required for one are the same skills required for the other. If we've helped you in either of those two areas, then this process has been successful."

The president explained how organizations that are successful over time must be composed of individually successful people. And those people, the president said, need to be successful at home and at work. The president encouraged the participants to continue in a lifelong pursuit of becoming more skilled in dealing with people. Then the final comment was, "You maximize your effectiveness when you do the right things, to the right people, at the right times."

When the speeches were over, it was the coach's turn. She stood at the front of the room and smiled at the managers. She began by saying, "This has been a great group to work with. I've really enjoyed our time together in class, as well as the one-on-

one sessions that I've had with each of you. I hope that you equally enjoyed this experience."

She said that the final session was mostly a celebration of their achievements for the past several months, but that she did have a few things she would like to review. Picking up a plastic bucket from a table, the coach held it up and continued, "You know about your feedback bucket and how important it is in your life. You know how you feel when it's full, and you know how you feel when it's empty. You've learned effective techniques to fill buckets, and you've practiced those techniques at work and at home."

The coach then picked up an ice pick from the table and said, "Some experiences in our lives create holes in our buckets." The coach jabbed the ice pick through the bottom of the bucket several times to make her point. She tilted the bucket so everyone could see the holes and then added, "Some of the holes are small, and some are large. We put some holes in ourselves, and we make choices to let other people put some in as well."

Once again she tilted the bucket on its side so that the people in the room could see what she had done to the bottom of the bucket. Then she put the bucket and ice pick on the table and walked to a position a little closer to the audience.

"When we began this process, it was my goal to awaken you to the power of supportive feedback, and the healing and changing effects of corrective feedback. I wanted each of you to know how ineffective insignificant feedback can be, and how damaging abusive feedback is. The feedback you give in any relationship either contributes to its success or contaminates it to failure. If you understand that message, then you are ready to graduate." The coach paused and gave the managers a big smile. Continuing she said, "Well, we're almost ready. All graduation ceremonies that I've attended have had a commencement speaker. And this one shouldn't be any different. Our panel of advisers has selected one of your graduates to be our commencement speaker. So,

Scott, would you please come over here and tell us what you've learned through this experience?"

There was applause from the managers as Scott's name was mentioned. Each person in the room knew how much Scott had learned and how far he had come since the day he was asked to get an envelope from the front desk. As he walked to the front of the room he seemed unsure what to say.

"This is a total surprise. I didn't know that I would be asked to say something, so I don't have anything prepared," he said.

A manager interrupted saying, "We planned it this way so your speech wouldn't last all day!"

After the laughter died down, Scott continued, "I really could go on for some time about what this experience has meant to me, my employees, and my family. But in the interest of time, I'll be brief."

Once again there was applause from the managers.

Scott's mood became more serious as he continued. "I can tell you that I deal with people differently now than I did before this class. I'm doing better with my employees. I know when and how to support their behaviors, and I know when and how to correct them. At times in the past I was abusive to people. I know that now. But now I work hard to prevent that from happening."

Scott broke his concentration and looked down toward the floor. Then he looked up at the coach and, with a quiver in his voice, added, "What most of you don't know is that my use of abusive feedback almost destroyed my relationship with my family. I came real close to losing my marriage. But thanks to this class, I'm fixing those problems too and I pledge to them, and to you, that it'll never happen again."

There was a brief pause and then everyone in the room rose to his or her feet to give Scott a standing ovation. Realizing that he was unable to say anything else, Scott slowly walked back to his seat while tears streamed down his face.

And as the celebration began, the coach, too, had tears in her eyes.

Time for a Vacation

After so many years of flying from one client to another, the coach had a routine in airports: Get in and get out. She had a tendency to keep her head down and walk quickly, pulling her wheeled suitcase from place to place, so it was only by luck that she happened to see Scott coming out of a gift shop.

"Hey there," Scott said. "You're walking pretty fast, young lady!"

"Scott, it's great to see you. I'm looking forward to our first session next month. I see that you've got fifteen new victims for the feedback process."

"We do. Hey, where are you headed?"

"I'm off for a session with another group. Where are you going?"

"It's not a business trip, finally. There won't be any ringing phones and employees saying, 'Hey, have you got a minute?'"

"It sounds like a vacation to me. Am I right?"

"That's right."

The coach could see a level of happiness in Scott's face that she hadn't seen before. She thought back to the first class where she had met him and recalled that she had questioned the boss's decision to use Scott as the retriever of the infamous envelope. Scott's reaction to denied feedback was typical, but the intensity of his response was a little disquieting. She could tell by his reaction that day that there were problems in his life. But as time went on, she could see great potential in his leadership abilities. She particularly liked his persistence and perseverance. So as she stood in the airport looking at this new Scott, she was pleased with the transformation that stood before her.

As the coach finished her thought, an attractive woman

walked up behind Scott and put her hand on his elbow. The woman smiled gently at the coach. Having made social blunders before, the coach waited to be introduced.

"Oh, I want you to meet my wife. Just the two of us are going for a week of sun, fun, and as I said, no phones. Honey, this is the consultant that I've told you so much about. I'll be her facilitator for the next group of managers in the feedback classes."

Scott's wife looked at the coach with a warm smile. "It's so nice to meet you. I've heard so much about you that it seems like we've been friends for years."

The coach was taken with her gentle and kind nature. And the way that she looked at Scott as she spoke said much about their current relationship. The coach said, "I'm so glad to see the two of you off on a vacation. It sounds absolutely wonderful. Even though I travel almost every week, I don't take the time to do that sun, fun, and no phones thing. I envy you!"

Scott's wife turned slightly to face the coach. She took her hand from Scott's elbow and placed it gently on the coach's hand. Her eyes were moist and her voice was soft as she said, "I can't begin to tell you how much your help has meant to both of us. You came into our lives at a point where we were about to make some very critical and damaging decisions. But because of what you taught Scott, and he in turn taught me, we are different people today than we were just a few months ago. Please accept my deepest thanks."

Scott, smiling, put his arm around his wife. The coach, her emotions on the surface, gained control and said, "I'm so glad that things are going well. I can tell that you are a great couple."

As the coach was about to turn away, Scott's wife had one final comment. "Thanks for the new Scott," she said.

They parted in front of the gift shop: Scott and his wife to a vacation, and the coach to another group of managers, but bearing a very full bucket herself.

Appendix

In Chapter 2 the coach administers an instrument (questionnaire) to the managers called the Feedback Assessment Inventory, so that they can quantify their existing skills in giving feedback. She administers the instrument early in her training process so that the managers are able to compare their abilities against a set of national norms. This comparison enables the managers to see a visual representation of their feedback skills on ten dimensions. The ten dimensions have been chosen because they encompass the broad abilities a person must have in order to give effective supportive and corrective feedback. The coach encourages the managers to periodically review their scores as an indicator of their strengths and weaknesses as they go through the feedback training process.

The instrument she uses in Chapter 2 (the Feedback Assessment Inventory) is included in this appendix. You can now complete the instrument by following the directions and then tabulate your scores with the self-scoring process. At that point you will be able to compare your existing abilities against those same national norms.

Although the technique was not used by the coach in the book, it would be possible for you to take the Feedback Assessment Inventory as a pretest, and then take it again as a posttest several months later to check your improvement. A second copy is contained at the end of this appendix.

It's important to remember that the results of your assessment can be no better than your objectivity and honesty in responding to each statement in the instrument. For this reason, it is strongly recommended that you read each item carefully and answer as honestly as possible.

Directions for Administration

This instrument contains thirty statements regarding how you give both supportive and/or corrective feedback to others. Before you begin the instrument, first reflect on how you give feedback to subordinates and colleagues. From that perspective, consider the accuracy of each statement. Then circle the appropriate letter for each statement, using the following key:

V = Very much like me
M = Mostly like me
S = Somewhat like me
N = Not at all like me

Feedback Assessment Inventory
Developed by Richard L. Williams, Ph.D.

1. When giving feedback, I rely on specific examples as a basis for the conversation.
   V   M   S   N

2. I try not to guess why a person did something; I concentrate on what was actually done.
    V   M   S   N

3. I focus on what the person did, not the personality or attitude.
    V   M   S   N

4. I give feedback as soon after the event as possible.
    V   M   S   N

5. I tell people what they did well in addition to what they did not do well.
    V   M   S   N

6. I work hard to not lose my cool or overreact when giving corrective feedback.
    V   M   S   N

7. I get to the point when giving feedback and don't ''beat around the bush.''
    V   M   S   N

8. I don't play ''gotcha'' by lying in wait for employees to make mistakes.
    V   M   S   N

9. When giving feedback, I describe how I feel about what happened.
    V   M   S   N

10. When giving corrective feedback, I encourage the other person to give his/her side of the situation.
    V   M   S   N

11. When giving corrective feedback I am aware of some possible solutions before the session begins.
    V   M   S   N

12. I use specific examples when giving feedback to make sure I'm very clear.
    V M S N

13. When giving feedback, I am behavior-oriented.
    V M S N

14. I give feedback at less stressful times, when the person and I are least likely to be rushed.
    V M S N

15. I believe a person deserves to know what he/she is doing right along with what needs to be improved.
    V M S N

16. I try to give corrective feedback when I can be calm and objective.
    V M S N

17. When giving feedback, I don't avoid eye contact, but make certain to look directly at the other person.
    V M S N

18. Giving feedback for me is an opportunity to help someone, not a time to get something off my chest.
    V M S N

19. I make sure I am communicating my feelings rather than blaming the other person.
    V M S N

20. When giving corrective feedback, I use paraphrasing and open-end questions to make sure I understand the situation.
    V M S N

21. I try to tailor or customize my feedback message specifically for the person.
    V M S N

22. I try to know what happened, rather than guess what happened.
    V M S N

23. When giving feedback, I try to avoid value labels like "irresponsible," "unprofessional," "good," or "bad."
    V M S N

24. I avoid giving negative or corrective feedback in public.
    V M S N

25. I try to be fair by balancing my use of supportive and corrective feedback.
    V M S N

26. When giving corrective feedback, I stick to the "here and now," and avoid long-past historical references.
    V M S N

27. When giving feedback, I stick to one or two high-priority issues.
    V M S N

28. When giving feedback, I don't offer advice unless the receiver asks for it.
    V M S N

29. When giving feedback, I describe how I feel so the receiver can understand the impact of the behavior being discussed.
    V M S N

30. When giving corrective feedback, I ask many questions to see the situation from the other person's perspective.
    V M S N

Scoring Part One

For scoring purposes your responses of "Very much like me," "Mostly like me," "Somewhat like me," and "Not at all like me" have numerical values. The values are as follows:

Very much like me = 3
Mostly like me = 2
Somewhat like me = 1
Not at all like me = 0

Scoring the Feedback Assessment Inventory is accomplished by adding the numerical values of three of the thirty items for each of the ten dimensions. For example, if you circled "Mostly like me" for item 1, then enter the numerical value of 2 following item 1 on the form below. And if you also circled "Mostly like me" on items 11 and 21, then enter the value of 2 for those items as well. Next, add the three item values horizontally for a total dimension score of 6 in the Total column. Now complete the following form to determine your total for each of the ten dimensions.

Dimensions	Items	Total
1. Have a plan.	1. ___ + 11. ___ + 21. ___	= ___
2. Be specific.	2. ___ + 12. ___ + 22. ___	= ___
3. Focus on behaviors.	3. ___ + 13. ___ + 23. ___	= ___
4. Time and place.	4. ___ + 14. ___ + 24. ___	= ___
5. Balanced feedback.	5. ___ + 15. ___ + 25. ___	= ___
6. Relevant feedback.	6. ___ + 16. ___ + 26. ___	= ___
7. Effective techniques.	7. ___ + 17. ___ + 27. ___	= ___
8. Effective style.	8. ___ + 18. ___ + 28. ___	= ___
9. Describe feelings.	9. ___ + 19. ___ + 29. ___	= ___
10. Listening skills.	10. ___ + 20. ___ + 30. ___	= ___

Scoring Part Two

The next step in scoring the Feedback Assessment Inventory is to transfer your ten dimensional scores to the graph on the following page. For example, take your total for dimension number one, "Have a plan," and transfer that number by placing a dot on the vertical scale representing dimension number one below. Then repeat that process for each of the remaining nine dimensions. After you have marked each dimension with a dot representing your total score above, draw a straight line from one dot to the next, creating a horizontal line graph.

Interpretation

Whenever a psychological instrument is administered and scored, there is a slight possibility of confusion or even inaccuracy. It's possible, for example, that the subject may have been less than truthful when completing the instrument. In a few situations the instrument itself may not give reliable data for certain subjects. This unique phenomenon is rare but may occur where the subject either doesn't understand the items as they were stated or may have confused the scoring values. A third reason is an incorrect tabulation of the scores. In any event, you may assume that the Feedback Assessment Inventory will give reliable data to more than 90 percent of respondents.

The display graph has a shaded band toward the top, which represents an ideal score (national norm) for each dimension. It is common for scores to have considerable variability from one dimension to another. You may, for example, have scores that range from high to low, depending on the dimension and your experience and skills in that area. Respondents who score in the shaded area typically have superior skills in delivering feedback in that dimension.

If your scores fall below the shaded area it does not mean that

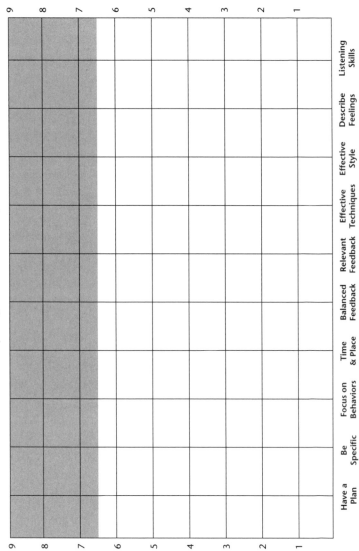

Feedback Assessment Inventory
Developed by Richard L. Williams, Ph.D.

you are incapable of delivering effective feedback. Rather, it merely means in that particular area you most likely have a need for improvement. It's important not to overreact to low scores, but instead to commit yourself to self-improvement. This book is an excellent source of skills and techniques to develop a realistic plan for improvement.

Feedback Assessment Inventory
Developed by Richard L. Williams, Ph.D.

1. When giving feedback, I rely on specific examples as a basis for the conversation.
   V M S N

2. I try not to guess why a person did something; I concentrate on what was actually done.
   V M S N

3. I focus on what the person did, not the personality or attitude.
   V M S N

4. I give feedback as soon after the event as possible.
   V M S N

5. I tell people what they did well in addition to what they did not do well.
   V M S N

6. I work hard to not lose my cool or overreact when giving corrective feedback.
   V M S N

7. I get to the point when giving feedback and don't "beat around the bush."
   V M S N

8. I don't play "gotcha" by lying in wait for employees to make mistakes.
   V M S N

9. When giving feedback, I describe how I feel about what happened.
   V M S N

10. When giving corrective feedback, I encourage the other person to give his/her side of the situation.
    V M S N

11. When giving corrective feedback I am aware of some possible solutions before the session begins.
    V M S N

12. I use specific examples when giving feedback to make sure I'm very clear.
    V M S N

13. When giving feedback, I am behavior-oriented.
    V M S N

14. I give feedback at less stressful times, when the person and I are least likely to be rushed.
    V M S N

15. I believe a person deserves to know what he/she is doing right along with what needs to be improved.
    V M S N

16. I try to give corrective feedback when I can be calm and objective.
    V M S N

17. When giving feedback, I don't avoid eye contact, but make certain to look directly at the other person.
    V M S N

18. Giving feedback for me is an opportunity to help someone, not a time to get something off my chest.
    V M S N

19. I make sure I am communicating my feelings rather than blaming the other person.
    V M S N

20. When giving corrective feedback, I use paraphrasing and open-end questions to make sure I understand the situation.
    V M S N

21. I try to tailor or customize my feedback message specifically for the person.
V   M   S   N

22. I try to know what happened, rather than guess what happened.
V   M   S   N

23. When giving feedback, I try to avoid value labels like "irresponsible," "unprofessional," "good," or "bad."
V   M   S   N

24. I avoid giving negative or corrective feedback in public.
V   M   S   N

25. I try to be fair by balancing my use of supportive and corrective feedback.
V   M   S   N

26. When giving corrective feedback, I stick to the "here and now," and avoid long-past historical references.
V   M   S   N

27. When giving feedback, I stick to one or two high-priority issues.
V   M   S   N

28. When giving feedback, I don't offer advice unless the receiver asks for it.
V   M   S   N

29. When giving feedback, I describe how I feel so the receiver can understand the impact of the behavior being discussed.
V   M   S   N

30. When giving corrective feedback, I ask many questions to see the situation from the other person's perspective.
V   M   S   N

Dimensions	Items	Total
1. Have a plan.	1. ___ + 11. ___ + 21. ___ =	___
2. Be specific.	2. ___ + 12. ___ + 22. ___ =	___
3. Focus on behaviors.	3. ___ + 13. ___ + 23. ___ =	___
4. Time and place.	4. ___ + 14. ___ + 24. ___ =	___
5. Balanced feedback.	5. ___ + 15. ___ + 25. ___ =	___
6. Relevant feedback.	6. ___ + 16. ___ + 26. ___ =	___
7. Effective techniques.	7. ___ + 17. ___ + 27. ___ =	___
8. Effective style.	8. ___ + 18. ___ + 28. ___ =	___
9. Describe feelings.	9. ___ + 19. ___ + 29. ___ =	___
10. Listening skills.	10. ___ + 20. ___ + 30. ___ =	___

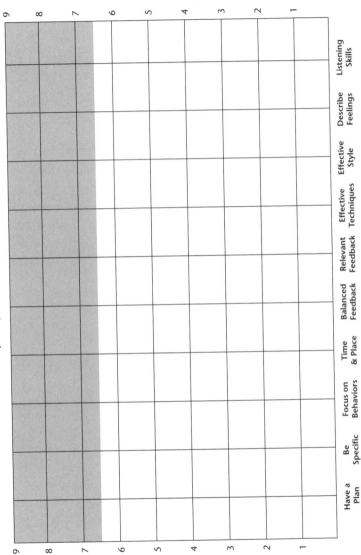

Feedback Assessment Inventory
Developed by Richard L. Williams, Ph.D.